TOUCHING

THE FACE

OF

GOD

40 Days of Adoring God

Gil Stieglitz

ISBN: 978-0-9831958-2-5
Theology/Spiritual Formation/Christian Living

Published by Thriving Churches Int'l, Inc., Minden, NV 89423
www.thrivingchurches.com

Cover Design by John Chase

Dedication

This book is dedicated to **Dr. Ken Townsend** who is my friend and fellow spiritual explorer. He goes deep with God and I am so blessed to know him. We have been exploring the wonder of God together for a very long time, and it has been a joy to know Him in this adventure.

Table of Contents

Introduction..8

Day 1: Adoration of God......................................11
Day 2: Essence: Infinite 12
Day 3: Essence: Self-Existent 14
Day 4: Essence: Spirit 16

Day 5: Attributes: Omniscient 18
Day 6: Attributes: Omnipotent............................22
Day 7: Attributes: Omnipresent 25
Day 8: Attributes: Immutable..............................27
Day 9: Attributes: Holiness................................29

Day 10: Attributes: Righteous/Just 32
Day 11: Attributes: Goodness 34
Day 12: Attributes: Longsuffering 37
Day 13: Attributes: Truth 39
Day 14: Attributes: Sovereignty.........................40

Day 15: Trinity...42
Day 16: Trinity: Jesus is called God 43
Day 17: Trinity: Holy Spirit is called God............45
Day 18: Names: Elohim, El Shaddai, Adonai, Yahweh.............46
Day 19: Names: Yahweh-Jireh, Yahweh-Rophe, Yahweh-
             M'Kaddesh, Yahweh-Shalom...................49

Day 20: Names: Shepherd, Judge, Yahweh-Elohim,
 Yahweh-Tsidkenu 51
Day 21: Names: Yahweh-Shammah, Yahweh-Saboath, El
 Elyon, Abhir, Kadosh 54
Day 22: Names: Shaphat, El Roi, Kanna, Palet, Yeshua 58
Day 23: Names: Gaol, Magen, Eyaluth, Tsaddiq, El-Olam........62
Day 24: Names: El-Gibhor, Zur, Sun of Righteousness,
 Attiq Yomim..66

Day 25: Names: Melekh, Angel of the Lord, Father, First
 and Last 71
Day 26: Names: Kurios, Theos, Despotes, I am, Theotes 76
Day 27: Names: Soter, Jesus, Christ...81
Day 28: Names: Shepherd of the Sheep, Master, King of
 Kings, Lord of Lords..84
Day 29: Names: Bishop and Guardian of our Souls,
 Deliverer, Adocate...88

Day 30: Names: Second Adam, Chief Cornerstone....................91
Day 31: Names: Immanuel, First Born, Head of the Body,
 Physician 93
Day 32: Names: Rock, Root of Jesse, Stone, Chief Apostle........97
Day 33: Names: Great High Priest, Author and Perfecter of
 our Faith 100
Day 34: Names: Lamb of God, Lamb Slain Before the
 Foundation of the World, Lord God Almighty,
 Logos, Sophia...102
Day 35: Names: Counselor, Comforter, Baptizer,
 Strengthener, Sanctifier, Spirit of Christ 107

Day 36: Names: The Seven-fold Spirit: Spirit of the Lord,
          Wisdom, Understanding, Counsel, Strength,
          Knowledge, Fear of the Lord, Spirit of Holiness 115
Day 37: Works: Creation...118
Day 38: Works: Exodus 120
Day 39: Works: Salvation 122
Day 40: Works: Scriptures 125
Day 41: Overall Gratefulness of God 126

Conclusion 127

Appendix: Why do we need to pray?.................................128

Small Group Materials..132

Preaching Materials 147

Introduction

Most people are fascinated by God but few are in relationship with Him. Even fewer of those who have embraced His gift of grace in His Son regularly push into His presence and enjoy deep fellowship. But God invites us through the apostles (1 John 1:1-3) to have our sins forgiven and a secure place in heaven. Come and learn how to praise God while learning about Him. This work has been thirty years in the making. I have used these praise exercises with all kinds of people over the years, and the result is always the same – a deeper understanding of God and entrance into the joy of His presence. Each time I practice these exercises -- whether individually or in a group -- it is as C.S. Lewis writes in His chronicles of Narnia -- "Further up and further in."

There is nothing like pushing into the presence of God. The way to do that is through praise, adoration, and exalting God. God Himself tells us that He dwells in the praises of His people (Psalm 22:3). Years ago, I invited two other men to join me in a unique time of prayer. I told them that we would be praising God and thanking God for as long as we could. I thought it would last twenty minutes at the most. We bowed our heads and began speaking the things that we knew of God in praise and adoration of Him. We thanked Him for everything in our lives. Each of us would pray for a few minutes while the others echoed what was said. Something wonderful began to happen. We were transported into the presence of God through our praise. I know that God is everywhere present, but somehow our focused praise made our awareness of God heightened and His presence more palpable. IT WAS WONDERFUL. When we finally stopped, three hours had passed and we all felt like we were walking three feet above the ground. Something had happened to all of us that had not happened to us before; we had been ushered into the presence and touched the face of God. I couldn't wait to do that again.

There are a number of different ways of praying through this book. You might start by committing to pray five minutes each day for 40 days, taking a different section each day. Some days you may pray for more than five minutes but other days just the five minutes. These prayer exercises are not meant to be a burden but to introduce you to the wonder of praising God. Each section in this book has more than enough material to last for five minutes.

Because there is more than enough material to praise God for five minutes, this book can be repeated over and over again praying the material that was not prayed the first time through. When a praise exercise asks you to write down things that you can praise God about, go ahead and write those things in the book. It will be tremendously encouraging the next time you go through the book to see what you wrote and to write down new ones you did not remember the last time through the book.

Some have even added these exercises as a regular part of their devotional time, repeatedly going through these praise exercises as a small part of their larger devotional time with the Lord.

Some have designated a particular day of the week that they will do these praise exercises, doing other prayer exercises on other days. This turns this book into 40 weeks of praise.

You might pray one of these sections per day for 40 days. This will take longer than five minutes each day, but it increases the spiritual adventure.

You might pray one of these sections for five minutes at the top of each hour during the typical work day.

You might pray one of these sections for five to ten minutes at 6am; 9am; 12 noon; 3pm; 6pm; 9pm.

Whichever level of involvement you choose for increasing your prayer life. You will see an increase in the answers and in the changes in your life and others. Don't miss this opportunity to connect to what God wants to do in your world through prayer.

Some churches have used this book for their small groups studies. Usually small groups use this material in two ways. One way is as a part of their small group time together, setting aside five to ten minutes to praise God using these praise exercises each time the group meets. This is a way to worship without singing and to learn about God in every group. A second way to use the material for small groups is to use these praise exercises as the focus of the group. This is where the whole group meets to praise God, using one or a number of the praise exercises. These praise sessions will last 30 minutes to an hour with everyone having pushed into the presence of God and been touched by Him.

Some churches use these praise exercises as a way to teach the doctrine of God. There are few things as dynamic as learning who God is by praising Him for each aspect of who He has revealed Himself to be.

Some churches even use this type of praise exercises as a way of praying for the worship services before and during the service itself. This is a powerful way of drawing God's presence and power to the large public services of the church.

Day 1: Adoration of God

Adore, glorify, exalt, honor, and magnify God for who He is:

He describes Himself in the Bible in terms of five aspects of His being:
- His Essence:
    - o Infinite, Self-Existent, Spirit
- His Attributes:
    - o Omniscient; Omnipresent; Omnipotent, Immutable
    - o Holy, Righteous, Good, Merciful, Longsuffering, Truth, Sovereign
- His Nature:
    - o Father, Son, and Holy Spirit
- His Names:
    - o God, Lord, Lord of Hosts, Most High, Jesus, Savior, Christ, I AM, Almighty, The Holy One
- His Works:
    - o Creation, Exodus, Bible, Salvation

Spend time magnifying God and adoring Him for who He describes Himself to be.

This whole book explores these aspects of the revelation of God in depth through praise, thanksgiving, and adoration.

Day 2: Essence: Infinite

The Essence of God
Infinite, Self-Existent, Spirit
He is the being above and beyond every other being. He is the one who has always existed and contains life within Himself. He is personal and pure spirit. Praise Him for who He is.

Essence: Infinite
- Thank God that He is eternal without beginning or end. Genesis 21:33

   Genesis 21:33
   Abraham planted a tamarisk tree at Beersheba, and there he called on the name of the LORD, the Everlasting God.

- Praise Him that He is so much more than the creator and caregiver of this small universe.
- Praise God that He is and was before any thought or atom of our universe.
- Thank God that He is beyond the boundaries of time and space. Isaiah 45:5-7

   Isaiah 45:5-7
   I am the LORD, and there is no other; Besides Me there is no God. I will gird you, though you have not known Me; that men may know from the rising to the setting of the sun that there is no one besides Me. I am the LORD, and there is no other, The One forming light and creating darkness, Causing well-being and creating calamity; I am the LORD who does all these.

- Praise God that He invented and has access to all dimensions of time and space and remains above them all.
- Praise God that He has access to dimensions of space and time so that He can be in complete control of everything and yet we have real, yet limited, freedom of the will.

Genesis 1:1
In the beginning God created the heavens and the earth.

- Marvel at God's creation and His designs for animals, plants, stars, insects, rocks, clouds.
- Exalt God for the natural laws He invented that govern the universe, the software He designed in each living being (DNA, RNA, etc), the wonder of the eco systems, and interconnectedness of life on this planet.
- Stand in awe and wonder at the stars, galaxies, and innumerable celestial bodies. God invented and created all that.

Jeremiah 23:24
"Can a man hide himself in hiding places so I do not see him?" declares the LORD. "Do I not fill the heavens and the earth?" declares the LORD.

Day 3: Essence: Self-Existent

Self-Existent Acts 17:24, 25
- Thank God that He is completely sufficient within Himself for all His needs

  Acts 17:24,25
  The God who made the world and all things in it, since He is Lord of heaven and earth, does not dwell in temples made with hands; nor is He served by human hands, as though He needed anything, since He Himself gives to all people life and breath and all things.

- Praise God that in the Tri-Unity of God He is perfectly loved, perfectly content, perfectly fulfilled, perfectly in harmony, and eternally sustained.
- Praise God that in His Trinity we understand the eternal source of love, communication, relationship, and purpose.
- Praise God that no human or angelic being can thwart God's plans or frustrate His internal harmony by being disobedient or rebellious.

  Isaiah 14:27
  For the LORD of hosts has planned, and who can frustrate it? And as for His stretched-out hand, who can turn it back?

- Praise God that He always has another way, another person, another option to accomplish His desires. He does not in any way need or depend upon any of us to accomplish His plan or make Him joyful.

- Praise God that He has chosen to extend the opportunity to us to be a part of His program, even though He has other ways.

2 Corinthians 3:5,6

Not that we are adequate in ourselves to consider anything as coming from ourselves, but our adequacy is from God,
who also made us adequate as servants of a new covenant, not of the letter but of the Spirit; for the letter kills, but the Spirit gives life.

- Thank God that He does not need anything from any part of His creation.
- Thank God that no one can put God in a position where He needs something.
- Thank God that you need Him but He doesn't need you. He wants to use you but He doesn't need you.

Day 4: Essence: Spirit

- Thank God that He is immaterial and incorporeal. Luke 24:39
- Thank God that He is invisible, not perceptible to our limited forms of visual or four-dimensional perceptions. John 1:18; 1 Timothy 1:17

1 Timothy 1:17
Now to the King eternal, immortal, invisible, the only God, be honor and glory forever and ever. Amen.

- Praise God that He is alive not dead or myth or a God from a past generation or only in Bible times. John 5:26; Psalm 36:9
- Praise Him that being alive He reacts to the world He created. He feels, interacts, and grieves the choices of His creation. While He knows everything that will happen, He is not an unfeeling, unreactive stoic being dispatching His orders without reaction or feeling.
- Praise God for His reactions to the situations, actions, problems, difficulties, and righteousnesses in our world.
- Allow your heart to be joyful over the things that bring joy to Him. Match the emotions of the Living God. Think about what brings Him joy.
- Allow your heart to be broken over the things that break His heart. Match the emotions of the Living God.
- Praise Him that as the Living God He acts into our world and any other worlds that He has created. He acts to keep His plan on track.

- Praise Him that He has not walked away from our broken sinful world, but that He still acts into it, bringing His living righteousness and holiness into our rebellious world.
- Praise Him that He is acting today to make sure that His purposes are accomplished.
- Give thanks to God that He is a person: self-conscious and self-determined; He is not the victim or prisoner of laws or others. Exodus 3:14

Exodus 3:14
God said to Moses, "I AM WHO I AM"; and He said, "Thus you shall say to the sons of Israel, 'I AM has sent me to you.'"

- Praise God that He wants an interactive personal relationship with you.
- Praise God that He has pursued you, initiating a relationship with you before you were ever interested or aware of His presence.
- Praise God that He knows you as a person and has chosen to love you and begin a relationship with you.
- Praise God that even though knowing all about you, He still wants a personal relationship with you and was willing to sacrifice His only Son to have it.

Day 5: Attributes: Omniscient

The Attributes of God
Omniscient, Omnipotent, Omnipresent, Immutable, Holy, Righteous, Good, Merciful, Longsuffering, Truth, Sovereign

God's attributes are the ways that His being acts. It is not proper to think of God separated into His attributes as though He was at one time love and another time wrath or a third time sovereign.

Omniscient
- Praise God that His knowledge is original, He thought up all that is and how it works. Isaiah 40:13,14

   Isaiah 40:13,14
   Who has directed the Spirit of the LORD, or as His counselor has informed Him?
   With whom did He consult and who gave Him understanding? And who taught Him in the path of justice and taught Him knowledge and informed Him of the way of understanding?

- Praise God that He is the Creator and inventor of everything; every form of life and every law that exists in our universe.
- He is also the creator and inventor of all the architecture that was required to bring our universe into existence.
- Praise God that He thought up all the different forms of life in our universe: bacteria, plant, insect, and animal, human. As well as the endless variety of each.
- Praise God for creating beauty and the ability to perceive it. He could have created a world that was only functional, but

instead He invested into this world what is true of Himself – beauty.

- He knows how to arrange and colorize things to create beauty, and He has done this over and over again throughout creation.
- Give Thanks to God that His knowledge is infallible. Isaiah 46:10
- Praise God that He knows everything about me and still has chosen to set His love upon me. Romans 5:8; Matthew 11:21; Psalm 139:1,2
- Praise God for His knowledge is instantaneous; He never has to look up any information, but the smallest fact is always available. Psalm 139:4

Psalm 139:1-6
O LORD, You have searched me and known me. You know when I sit down and when I rise up; You understand my thought from afar. You scrutinize my path and my lying down, and are intimately acquainted with all my ways. Even before there is a word on my tongue, Behold, O LORD, You know it all. You have enclosed me behind and before, and laid Your hand upon me. Such knowledge is too wonderful for me; it is too high, I cannot attain to it.

- Praise God that He will never be surprised by anything I do or say or think: He knows me completely. Psalm 139:1-5
- Praise God that His knowledge is so complete that He knows everything that I am thinking even before I think it. Psalm 139:1-4
- Praise God that He knows every possible choice of every man and every choice that could come from even possible choices and yet is not responsible for the sinful choices of any man. Matthew 11:21,23

- Adore God that His knowledge is retained; He never forgets anything or loses info except what He chooses not to know. Hebrews 6:10; Psalm 50:21
- Praise God that His knowledge is exhaustive; He will never be surprised by a discovery or invention. Ezekiel 11:5; Job 21:22
- Praise God that He has specifically designed each person for a glorifying purpose in this world and leaves obvious clues as to what that purpose is. Psalm 139:13-15

Psalm 139:13-16
For You formed my inward parts; You wove me in my mother''s womb. I will give thanks to You, for I am fearfully and wonderfully made; Wonderful are Your works, and my soul knows it very well. My frame was not hidden from You, When I was made in secret, and skillfully wrought in the depths of the earth; Your eyes have seen my unformed substance; And in Your book were all written the days that were ordained for me, when as yet there was not one of them.

- Praise God that even when a person chooses to rebel from God, He has the knowledge and wisdom to turn their rebellion into an exaltation of His glory. Proverbs 16:4; Romans 9:22
- Adore God that He knows every possibility of every possibility. Matthew 11:21
- Praise God that His knowledge is infinite; we will never know as much as God; there is nothing that can be known in any possible world or any possible timeline that He does not already know. Revelation 1:8
- Praise God that He is the All Wise God. Romans 16:27

- Praise God that we see His wisdom In His works of Creation. Proverbs 8:22-30
- Praise God that we see His wisdom in His works of Providence. Genesis 50:20

Genesis 50:20
"As for you, you meant evil against me, but God meant it for good in order to bring about this present result, to preserve many people alive."

- Praise God that we see His wisdom in His work of Redemption. Ephesians 3:10-14

Day 6: Attributes: Omnipotent

Omnipotent Job 9:4
- Praise God that He is All Powerful and has All Authority.
- Praise God that He and He alone can do whatever He wants. Psalm 115:3

Psalm 115:3
But our God is in the heavens; He does whatever He pleases.

- Praise God that in His power He is not capricious or arbitrary but controlled by His righteous, justice and holiness.
- Praise God for the Immensity of His Creation which displays His power. Isaiah 44:24
- Give thanks for the fact that God does at times display His power to counteract the normal flow of this universe.
- Praise God that he heals when the universe decrees sickness.
- Praise God that He supplies when our choices and the world system decrees poverty.
- Praise God that He forgives and reconciles when man's laws and the universe would demand justice, wrath, and hatred.
- Praise God that He redirects the affairs of mankind in answer to prayer and for His own purposes to accomplish His goals.
- Praise God that He exerts His power in answer to the prayers of His people. Luke 18:1-10
- Praise God that He does not answer all of the prayers of His people. James 4:1-4
- Praise God that He has All Authority.
- Give thanks to God that His right to rule is established by the perfections of His nature (wisdom, righteousness,

goodness, holiness, faithfulness and truth), not by the extent of his power. Exodus 34:5-8; Psalm 93:1,2; Revelation 4:11

Revelation 4:11

Worthy are You, our Lord and our God, to receive glory and honor and power; for You created all things, and because of Your will they existed, and were created.

- Give God thanks that His style of exercising His authority is not autocratic, dictatorial, micro- management, or laissez faire but that of a caring shepherd.
- Praise God that He has made humans in His image and according to His likeness with the ability to choose to stay within moral boundaries rather than being governed by instincts as animals.
- Give adoration to God that He delegates His authority to angels, mankind, and various other living things to exercise His authority in their realms.
- Adore God that He has given mankind His authority in their affairs to build a civilization that dwells in peace, safety, and prosperity.
- Weep as mankind has corrupted God's authority to serve their own individual purposes and harm their own kind.
- Praise God that He by His power and His authority has developed a wonderful plan for each human being, taking into account who He has made them and the circumstances of their situation. Acts 17:24-26; Psalm 139:13-15
- Adore God that no one can escape from God's authority. Everyone will ultimately acknowledge that God is Lord of All. Romans 1:18

Romans 1:18

For the wrath of God is revealed from heaven against all ungodliness and unrighteousness of men who suppress the truth in unrighteousness

- Praise God that no rebellion can or will succeed – either angelic or human. Revelation 12:9, 20:9
- Praise God that nothing can take place except that He gives or has given his permission for it to take place. Matthew 10:29

Day 7: Attributes: Omnipresent

Praise God that He is everywhere present; that no one can ever flee from His penetrating presence or gaze. Psalm 139:7-12

> **Psalm 139:7-12**
> *Where can I go from Your Spirit? Or where can I flee from Your presence? If I ascend to heaven, You are there; If I make my bed in Sheol, behold, You are there. If I take the wings of the dawn, if I dwell in the remotest part of the sea, even there Your hand will lead me, and Your right hand will lay hold of me. If I say, "Surely the darkness will overwhelm me, and the light around me will be night," Even the darkness is not dark to You, and the night is as bright as the day. Darkness and light are alike to You.*

- Praise God that it is not His size that makes Him Omnipresent. It is the nature of His spirit being and eternity in which He dwells.
- Praise God that our universe is not His universe or the whole of His focus.
- Praise God that He is with you right now.
- Praise God that there is no reason why He should be concerned with puny human creatures that crawl upon a planet away in one of billions of galaxies, but He does take notice of mankind and you as a person. Your choices and worship and thoughts are of deep concern to Him.
- Be overwhelmed by God's presence in, around, and over you. He knows every thought that will drift through your mind and which ones you will grasp and dwell on. There is not a place you can go that the penetrating gaze and

presence of God does not know you. There is no privacy
from Him.
- Praise God that His presence around you sees and knows
everything that you are doing.

Proverbs 15:3
*The eyes of the LORD are in every place, watching
the evil and the good.*

- Praise God that He has not lost sight or track of you; He
knows right where you are whether you are in His will or
not
- Praise God that He right now is nearer to you than anyone
else could be and knows more about you than you know
about yourself and wants to be gracious, merciful, and
powerfully loving to you.

Day 8: Attributes: Immutable

- Praise God that the perfections of His nature do not change. Malachi 3:6; Psalms 102:25-27

Psalms 102:25-27
Of old You founded the earth, and the heavens are the work of Your hands. Even they will perish, but You endure; and all of them will wear out like a garment; like clothing You will change them and they will be changed. But You are the same, and Your years will not come to an end.

- Praise God that He will continue to love.
- Praise God that He will continue to honor the promises that He has made in His word to me.
- Praise God that the way that He treated Abram, David, and Jeremiah is the way that He will treat me.

Malachi 3:6
For I, the LORD, do not change; therefore you, O sons of Jacob, are not consumed.

- Praise God that at some time in the future He will not grow tired of me and discard me or refuse to love me. He is unchanging.
- Praise God that the same Jesus that came to display the glory of the Father (and was so unexpected and gentle) is the same Jesus that I will meet face to face in heaven. Hebrews 13:8

Hebrews 13:8
Jesus Christ is the same yesterday and today and forever.

- Praise God that any change in God's interaction with me is not from His end but is a corruption on my side.
- Praise God that His wonderful plan for my life has not changed. The same talents, gifts, and desires that He placed in me long ago are still waiting to be fulfilled through my obedience to Him. He wants me to live a life that is fully alive. I am making the wrong turns not Him.
- Praise God that He keeps His covenants. Numbers 23:19

Numbers 23:19
God is not a man, that He should lie, nor a son of man, that He should repent; has He said, and will He not do it? Or has He spoken, and will He not make it good?

- Praise God that He remembers and keeps His promises.
- Praise God that He is not arbitrary or capricious. James 1:17; Hebrews 13:8

James 1:17
Every good thing given and every perfect gift is from above, coming down from the Father of lights, with whom there is no variation or shifting shadow.

Day 9: Attributes: Holiness

- Give thanks to God that He is pure; that He is not corrupted by sin, selfishness, or a violation of His own perfections; and He can never become corrupted Psalm 29:2; 1 Peter 1:14-16

1 Peter 1:14-16
As obedient children, do not be conformed to the former lusts which were yours in your ignorance, but like the Holy One who called you, be holy yourselves also in all your behavior; because it is written, "YOU SHALL BE HOLY, FOR I AM HOLY."

- Adore the Transcendent God who is above all, over all, and through all. He is so far beyond any created thing that to contemplate Him is only an approximation and is significant in comparison to all that He is. Exodus 15:11; Isaiah 6:1-5

Exodus 15:11
Who is like You among the gods, O LORD? Who is like You, majestic in holiness, awesome in praises, working wonders?

- Praise God that He is beyond any mental conception that we can have of Him. Not that every conception is false; it is incomplete and beneath Him.
- Fear the Lord God the Holy One who stands as truly terrible and Other than any created being.
- We should be deeply afraid of offending this Holy Being.

Isaiah 6:1-5

In the year of King Uzziah"s death I saw the Lord sitting on a throne, lofty and exalted, with the train of His robe filling the temple. Seraphim stood above Him, each having six wings: with two he covered his face, and with two he covered his feet, and with two he flew. And one called out to another and said, "Holy, Holy, Holy, is the LORD of hosts, the whole earth is full of His glory." And the foundations of the thresholds trembled at the voice of him who called out, while the temple was filling with smoke. Then I said, "Woe is me, for I am ruined! Because I am a man of unclean lips, And I live among a people of unclean lips; for my eyes have seen the King, the LORD of hosts."

- Praise God that we have no conception of the dimensionality in which He dwells -- if it is a dimensionality at all.
- My every thought of God is in some way a corruption of who He really is. What He has communicated in the Scriptures is as much as we can bear or comprehend of who He is.
- Praise God that the angels who are superior in might, power, and knowledge to us are still infinitesimally distant from the wonder and Otherness of God. They shout Holy, Holy, Holy.
- Be awestruck by the Transcendence of God who can create the vastness of the Universe and the intricacies of the human body and cells. Let yourself be staggered by the one who thought this all up.
- Holiness also means God is Pure.
- Give thanks to God that He is pure; that He is not corrupted by sin, selfishness, or a violation of His own perfections; and He can never become corrupted. Psalm 29:2; 1 Peter 1:14-16

Revelation 4:8

And the four living creatures, each one of them having six wings, are full of eyes around and within; and day and night they do not cease to say, "HOLY, HOLY, HOLY is THE LORD GOD, THE ALMIGHTY, WHO WAS AND WHO IS AND WHO IS TO COME."

Day 10: Attributes: Righteous/Just

- Praise God that He is always right in His decisions, judgments, character, and works. Deuteronomy 32:4; Psalm 19:9

Deuteronomy 32:4
The Rock! His work is perfect, for all His ways are just; A God of faithfulness and without injustice, Righteous, and upright is He.

- Give thanks to God that no one can escape from His authority. Romans 1:18; Psalm 58:11; Psalm 75:7; Hebrews 11:6
- Praise God that the Judge of all the earth shall do right. Genesis 18:25
- Give thanks that God's decisions are always right even though from our limited space-time perspective they do not always seem that way. We can put our trust in Him. Psalm 19:9

Psalm 19:9b
The judgments of the LORD are true; they are righteous altogether.

- Praise God that His justice and righteousness will not allow the guilty to go unpunished.
- Praise God that those who turn away from Him and refuse His mercy and forgiveness will be rewarded appropriately for their rebellion.
- Give thanks to God that even when man cannot think of a right way to move forward, there is still a right action that God knows.

1 Peter 1:17
If you address as Father the One who impartially judges according to each one"s work, conduct yourselves in fear during the time of your stay on earth.

- Praise God that one day the wrath of God will be full and those who deserve justice will receive it in full measure.

Day 11: Attributes: Goodness

- Praise God that He is the ultimate Goal of life. When we seek Him we will not be disappointed. Psalm 34:8,10; Exodus 33:19;

Psalm 34:8,10
O taste and see that the LORD is good; how blessed is the man who takes refuge in Him! The young lions do lack and suffer hunger; but they who seek the LORD shall not be in want of any good thing.

- Praise God that we will one day be swallowed up by the ultimate good, never to be a part of a sinful world again.

Psalm 16:11
You will make known to me the path of life; In Your presence is fullness of joy; In Your right hand there are pleasures forever.

- Praise God that He is Love. Adore God that He meets our deepest needs, pursues us when we are His enemies, and even pleases us with special favors and blessings we do not deserve. 1 John 3:1; 1 John 4:9-11

1 John 4:9-11
By this the love of God was manifested in us, that God has sent His only begotten Son into the world so that we might live through Him. In this is love, not that we loved God, but that He loved us and sent His Son to be the propitiation for our sins. Beloved, if God so loved us, we also ought to love one another.

- Praise God that while we were still sinners Christ died for us out of His great love for us.
- Praise God that nothing can separate us from the Love of God. He loves us with an unshakeable love. Romans 8:31-39

Romans 8:31-39

What then shall we say to these things? If God is for us, who is against us? He who did not spare His own Son, but delivered Him over for us all, how will He not also with Him freely give us all things? Who will bring a charge against God's elect? God is the one who justifies; who is the one who condemns? Christ Jesus is He who died, yes, rather who was raised, who is at the right hand of God, who also intercedes for us. Who will separate us from the love of Christ? Will tribulation, or distress, or persecution, or famine, or nakedness, or peril, or sword? Just as it is written, "FOR YOUR SAKE WE ARE BEING PUT TO DEATH ALL DAY LONG; WE WERE CONSIDERED AS SHEEP TO BE SLAUGHTERED." But in all these things we overwhelmingly conquer through Him who loved us. For I am convinced that neither death, nor life, nor angels, nor principalities, nor things present, nor things to come, nor powers, nor height, nor depth, nor any other created thing, will be able to separate us from the love of God, which is in Christ Jesus our Lord.

- Praise God that He is Gracious; giving to us blessings, power, desire, and supplies we do not deserve nor could ever earn. Romans 5:1,2

- Give thanks to God that He is Merciful; not demanding the full measure of our punishment from us.
- Praise God that He protects us from some of the consequences of our actions. Psalm 86:15

Day 12: Attributes: Longsuffering

- Give thanks to God that He is patient and longsuffering with us. Genesis 6:3; Romans 2:4

Romans 2:4
Or do you think lightly of the riches of His kindness and tolerance and patience, not knowing that the kindness of God leads you to repentance?

- Give thanks to God that He is willing to put up with our rebellion and selfishness in order to accomplish His purpose.
- Praise God that He has factored in our stubbornness and rebellion so that His plan is in no way affected by our lack of cooperation.
- Give thanks that God is not like you – who would have given up hope on yourself and others long before this.
- Marvel at God for being willing to put up with the insults, rebellion, disobedience, and lack of faith that comes from humanity in order to collect a people who would love Him.
- Thank God for the ways that He is patient and longsuffering with you. Name the specific areas where you have been slow to change, act, grow, and redirect yourself to be in line with His will.
- Thank Him that He has not said, "I have had enough of this world and your sins!!!"

2 Peter 3:9
The Lord is not slow about His promise, as some count slowness, but is patient toward you, not wishing for any to perish but for all to come to repentance.

- Thank God that no matter how long it could take, He has a plan to restore and use you for His purposes.
- Praise God that He is longsuffering in His anger at our sinfulness and rebellion.

Day 13: Attributes: Truth

- Give thanks to God that He is the truth in an ultimate sense that when all is over there will be God. Isaiah 44:8,9

Isaiah 44:24
Thus says the LORD, your Redeemer, and the one who formed you from the womb, "I, the LORD, am the maker of all things, Stretching out the heavens by Myself and spreading out the earth all alone."

- Praise God that He communicates truly; He does not deceive us or hide the truth from us. Hebrews 6:17,18; John 17:17

John 17:17
Sanctify them in the truth; Your word is truth.

Day 14: Attributes: Sovereignty

- Praise God that He is in control of the whole of His creation in every way. Nothing happens without His understanding and approval. Daniel 4:35

Daniel 4:35
All the inhabitants of the earth are accounted as nothing, But He does according to His will in the host of heaven and among the inhabitants of earth; and no one can ward off His hand or say to Him, "What have You done?"

- Adore God because His sovereignty is based upon the perfections of His being not His power or will. Exodus 34:6,7

Exodus 34:6,7
Then the LORD passed by in front of him and proclaimed, "The LORD, the LORD God, compassionate and gracious, slow to anger, and abounding in lovingkindness and truth; who keeps lovingkindness for thousands, who forgives iniquity, transgression and sin; yet He will by no means leave the guilty unpunished, visiting the iniquity of fathers on the children and on the grandchildren to the third and fourth generations."

- Give thanks to God for His providence that directs, controls, guides, redirects, and puts boundaries around everything. 1 Chronicles 29:11; Psalm 115:3; Isaiah 45:9

1 Chronicles 29:11,12

Yours, O LORD, is the greatness and the power and the glory and the victory and the majesty, indeed everything that is in the heavens and the earth; Yours is the dominion, O LORD, and You exalt Yourself as head over all.

Both riches and honor come from You, and You rule over all, and in Your hand is power and might; and it lies in Your hand to make great and to strengthen everyone.

- Praise God that He sustains, upholds and preserves; He does not allow our universe to fly apart but upholds it. Colossians 1:17; Hebrews 1:3
- Praise God that He has made a distinction between the inevitable and those who will commit the inevitable. Matthew 18:7

Day 15: Trinity

The Nature of God: Trinity
God describes Himself as Eternal Father, Eternal Son, and Eternal Spirit. He is a Tri-une being, above and beyond our comprehension. We can grasp the truth of who He is and we are driven to praise and stand in awe.

Tri-une: Father: Son: Holy Spirit
- Praise God that He is the eternally existing Tri-une God: completely self-sufficient in love within Himself.

    Genesis 1:26
    Then God said, "Let Us make man in Our image, according to Our likeness."

- Praise God for the Oneness that exists within the separate personal distinctions of the Godhead.
- Praise God that individuality is still present in God. Uniqueness and diversity are not eliminated.
- Praise God for the eternal love between Father, Son, and Holy Spirit that sustains them and models for us true love.
- All three are linked as God: Matthew 28:19
- Praise God that He has been extremely clear that He dwells on a plane of being where it is possible to have three distinct personalities in one being.

    Matthew 28:19
    Go therefore and make disciples of all the nations, baptizing them in the name of the Father and the Son and the Holy Spirit.

Day 16: Trinity: Jesus is called God

John 1:1-4,14

In the beginning was the Word, and the Word was with God, and the Word was God. He was in the beginning with God. All things came into being through Him, and apart from Him nothing came into being that has come into being. In Him was life, and the life was the Light of men.

And the Word became flesh, and dwelt among us, and we saw His glory, glory as of the only begotten from the Father, full of grace and truth.

- Praise God for the eternal Son of God who became a man -- Jesus of Nazareth -- that He might pay for our debt of sin.
- Praise God that in eternity past a distinction was wrought within the Oneness of God called the Son -- begotten not made.
- Praise God that the Son was willing to lay aside His equality in the Godhead and assume the role of a servant and Savior.
- Praise God that God the Son was willing to become a human, live a perfect life without the aid of His divinity, and offer that life as a payment for sin.

Colossians1:13-20

For He rescued us from the domain of darkness, and transferred us to the kingdom of His beloved Son, in whom we have redemption, the forgiveness of sins. He is the image of the invisible God, the firstborn of all creation. For by Him all things were created, both in the heavens and on earth, visible and invisible, whether thrones or dominions or rulers or authorities—all things have been created through Him and for Him. He is before all things, and in Him all things hold together. He is also head of the body, the church; and He is the beginning, the firstborn from the dead, so that He Himself will come to have first place in everything. For it was the Father"s good pleasure for all the fullness to dwell in Him, and through Him to reconcile all things to Himself, having made peace through the blood of His cross; through Him, I say, whether things on earth or things in heaven.

Day 17: Trinity: Holy Spirit is called God

Holy Spirit is called God: Acts 5:3-4
- Praise God that the perfection of the Spirit of God was and is willing to minister to sinful mankind to bring about the redemption of mankind.

Genesis 1:2
The earth was formless and void, and darkness was over the surface of the deep, and the Spirit of God was moving over the surface of the waters.

- Praise God that the only truly Holy Spirit gives gifts to men to help them minister the power of Christ. 1 Corinthians 12:4

1 Corinthians 12:4
Now there are varieties of gifts, but the same Spirit.

- Praise God that the Holy Spirit prays when we do not know what to pray and can only groan over our troubles and limited perspective. Romans 8:26

Romans 8:26
In the same way the Spirit also helps our weakness; for we do not know how to pray as we should, but the Spirit Himself intercedes for us with groanings too deep for words.

Day 18: Names: Elohim, El Shaddai, Adonai, Yahweh

The Names of God

Give thanks and praise to God for the fact that each of these names is true of God. Look at each name and think of a situation where God was this to you.

ELOHIM: God as "Creator, Preserver, Transcendent, Mighty, and Strong" Genesis 1:1; 17:7, 6:18, 9:15, 50:24; 1 Kings 8:23

> **Genesis 1:1**
> *In the beginning God created the heavens and the earth.*

- Praise God that he is the Creator, Preserver, and Mighty God who called the world into being.

EL SHADDAI: "God All-Sufficient" Genesis 17:1,2
In Revelation 16:7, Lord God the Almighty.

> **Genesis 17:2**
> *Now when Abram was ninety-nine years old, the LORD appeared to Abram and said to him, "I am God Almighty; walk before Me, and be blameless."*

- Praise God that He is the all-sufficient one who commands all the angels and all the universe. He is the Lord God Almighty

ADONAI: "Lord" in our English Bibles: first use of Adonai Genesis 15:2; 2 Samuel 7:18-22

2 Samuel 7:18-22
Then David the king went in and sat before the LORD, and he said, "Who am I, O Lord GOD, and what is my house, that You have brought me this far? And yet this was insignificant in Your eyes, O Lord GOD, for You have spoken also of the house of Your servant concerning the distant future. And this is the custom of man, O Lord GOD. Again what more can David say to You? For You know Your servant, O Lord GOD! For the sake of Your word, and according to Your own heart, You have done all this greatness to let Your servant know. For this reason You are great, O Lord GOD; for there is none like You, and there is no God besides You, according to all that we have heard with our ears."

•   Praise God that He is the one in charge, the Lord. He is the most worthy to be in charge because of the perfections of His being. No one else could truly earn supremacy as Lord.

YAHWEH: Yahweh is the covenant name of God. From the verb "to be," havah, similar to chavah (to live), "The Self-Existent One" Exodus 3:14. This is the personal name of God that He shares with those He invites into covenant with Him.

Exodus 3:14
God said to Moses, "I AM WHO I AM"; and He said, "Thus you shall say to the sons of Israel, 'I AM has sent me to you.'"

•   Praise God that He has revealed himself as the ever living one who dwells in the present.

John 8:58

Jesus said to them, "Truly, truly, I say to you, before Abraham was born, I am."

Day 19: Names: Yahweh-Jireh, Yahweh-Rophe, Yahweh-M'Kaddesh, Yahweh-Shalom

YAHWEH-JIREH: "The Lord will Provide" Genesis 22:14

Genesis 22:14
Abraham called the name of that place The LORD Will Provide, as it is said to this day, "In the mount of the LORD it will be provided."

- Praise God that He will always provide for His worshippers. He is the one who knows and will see that what is needed is on its way or at the right place at the right time.
- Think back on three specific times that God provided for you. Take the time to write down what He did and thank Him for it.

1.

2.

3.

YAHWEH-ROPHE: "The Lord Who Heals" Exodus 15:22-26
- God is a healing God. He delights to bring mental, physical, spiritual, emotional, and relational healing to your life. Thank Him for His willingness to do that and the times He has done that for you.

Exodus 15:26
And He said, "If you will give earnest heed to the voice of the LORD your God, and do what is right in His sight, and give ear to His commandments, and keep all His statutes, I will put none of the diseases on you which I have put on the Egyptians; for I, the LORD, am your healer."

YAHWEH-M'KADDESH: "The Lord Who Sanctifies" Leviticus 20:8. "To make whole, set apart for holiness."

Leviticus 20:8
You shall keep My statutes and practice them; I am the LORD who sanctifies you.

YAHWEH-SHALOM: "The Lord Our Peace" Judges 6:24. "Shalom" translated "peace" 170 times means "whole," "finished," "fulfilled."

Judges 6:24
Then Gideon built an altar there to the LORD and named it The LORD is Peace.

Day 20: Names: Shepherd, Judge, Yahweh-Elohim, Yahweh-Tsidkenu

SHEPHERD: Psalm 23; **YAHWEH-ROHI:** Isaiah 40:11
"The Lord Our Shepherd"

Psalm 23
The LORD is my shepherd, I shall not want. He makes me lie down in green pastures; He leads me beside quiet waters. He restores my soul; He guides me in the paths of righteousness For His name"s sake. Even though I walk through the valley of the shadow of death, I fear no evil, for You are with me; Your rod and Your staff, they comfort me. You prepare a table before me in the presence of my enemies; You have anointed my head with oil; My cup overflows. Surely goodness and lovingkindness will follow me all the days of my life, and I will dwell in the house of the LORD forever.

Write down five specific times in your life when God has shepherded you and then praise Him out loud for those times.

1.

2.

3.

4.

5.

JUDGE: Psalm 7:18, 96:13

- God is and will be our judge. It does not matter what we think or what others think of our actions, thoughts, or words; but it does matter what God thinks.
- Exalt Him for comprehensive nature of His judgment.
- Thank Him that He will know all when He Judges.
- Thank Him that no one will escape His justice.
- Thank Him that He is a judge with mercy for those who accept His provision.
- Tremble at His judgment of you – every thought, every word, and every action. Remind yourself of your need for His mercy offered in Jesus Christ.
-

YAHWEH-ELOHIM: "LORD God" Genesis 2:4

- Thank God that He has let us known His personal name – Yahweh. He has not remained far off and distant from us in His creation. He has come to interact and communicate with us.
- Give Him praise that He is a personal God who would want us to know His name.
- Praise God that He is not just powerful – Elohim – but also personal Yahweh.
- Exalt God that He is the full embodiment of His name: Life itself and the Supreme Being.

YAHWEH-TSIDKENU: "The Lord Our Righteousness" Jeremiah 23:5, 6, 33:16

- Praise God that He can rightly be called "The Lord our Righteousness." There is no hypocrisy in that title.
- Exalt God that He is righteous and has not done anything that is a mistake or evil.

- Praise God that while we are not righteous He is righteous and He offers His perfect righteousness to us.
- Rejoice that even though the world, the flesh, and the devil remind you of your unrighteousness, God is your righteousness. He offers to us what we could not be on our own – righteous perfection enough to move into the presence of God.
- Announce to the world, the flesh, and the devil that God has offered to be your righteousness and you have accepted.
- Thank God for His offer of His perfect righteousness and reassert your desire to have His righteousness rather than your own.

Jeremiah 33:16
'In those days Judah will be saved and Jerusalem will dwell in safety; and this is the name by which she will be called: the LORD is our righteousness.'

Day 21: Names: Yahweh-Shammah, Yahweh-Saboath, El Elyon, Abhir, Kadosh

YAHWEH-SHAMMAH: "The Lord is There" Ezekial 48:35

- Ezekiel celebrates that one day there will be a city which will be called the Lord is There. God will dwell in one city among mankind. This will be heaven or the heavenly city.
- Praise God that one day He will dwell with us and we will be living in the city set up by Him, run by Him, and full of Him.
- Praise God that His plan to redeem mankind and have them dwell with Him will be brought to completion.
- Praise God that while at times in this life God is hidden and understanding what He is up to is like looking through a smudged window, one day we will be in His presence and we will live in the city which is called the Lord is There.

YAHWEH-SABAOTH: "The Lord of Hosts" The commander of the angelic host and the armies of God. Isaiah 1:24; 2 Kings 3:9-12

- Praise God that He is the unquestioned commander of all the Holy angels.

  Isaiah 1:24
  Therefore the Lord GOD of hosts, The Mighty One of Israel, declares, "Ah, I will be relieved of My adversaries and avenge Myself on My foes.

- When God's patience has run out and He comes to set the world right, He will come with all the Holy Angels as their commander.

2 Thessalonians 1:7,8
...and to give relief to you who are afflicted and to us as well when the Lord Jesus will be revealed from heaven with His mighty angels in flaming fire, dealing out retribution to those who do not know God and to those who do not obey the gospel of our Lord Jesus.

- Praise God that when He orders the angels to aid His people, they jump to obey His orders. Hebrews 1:14
- Praise God that He has assigned angels to us; angels who watch for His orders to assist, protect, and defend us. Psalm 37:4; Matthew 18:10

EL ELYON: "Most High" (from "to go up") Deuteronomy 26:19, 32:8; Psalm 18:13; Genesis 14:18

Genesis 14:19-20
He blessed him and said, "Blessed be Abram of God Most High, possessor of heaven and earth; and blessed be God Most High, who has delivered your enemies into your hand." He gave him a tenth of all.

- Praise God that He is the God Most High. There are no other gods above Him or any being equal to Him. He is the Supreme One. He is the God above all so-called gods.
- Praise God that there will never be a more powerful being disagreeing or countermanding what God has said.
- Give Thanks to God that while others worship what will be revealed as insignificant and low ranking demons, He has invited you to worship Him who is above and beyond every other being.

- Praise God that He has saved you from worshipping a false god or phony goal. You have been given insight to pursue the one true God.

ABHIR: "Mighty One" Genesis 49:24; Deuteronomy 10:17

Genesis 49:24
But his bow remained firm, and his arms were agile, from the hands of the Mighty One of Jacob (From there is the Shepherd, the Stone of Israel).

- Praise God that He is has demonstrated that He is mighty in history. Write down your favorite Bible story of God's display of His might in history.

1. Creation

2. Exodus

3. Deliverance of Gideon against the Midianites

4. David and Goliath

5. Peter's deliverance from jail

6.

7.

8.

9.

10.

- Praise God for three specific times that He has demonstrated Himself mighty for you.

    1.

    2.

    3.

KADOSH: "Holy One" Psalm 71:22; Isaiah 40:25
- Praise God that He is the Holy One: He is transcendent and completely pure.
- Stand in awe that the God that you worship is the completely different being who stands completely apart from every part of His creation. There is nothing in Creation to which you can compare Him. He is totally different, above and beyond. The whole of creation came from His mind and His handiwork.

    Psalm 71:22
    I will also praise You with a harp, even Your truth,
    O my God; To You I will sing praises with the lyre,
    O Holy One of Israel.

Day 22: Names: Shaphat, El Roi, Kanna, Palet, Yeshua

SHAPHAT: "Judge" Genesis 18:25

- There are many things that do not make sense to us on this side of heaven, but our great answer is that we serve the God who does right.
- Praise God that He who is the judge will do right.

   Genesis 18:25
   Far be it from You to do such a thing, to slay the righteous with the wicked, so that the righteous and the wicked are treated alike. Far be it from You! Shall not the Judge of all the earth deal justly?

- Thank God for the times when you have followed His guidance and watched Him make the right happen.

   1.

   2.

   3.

- Praise God for the times when it looked like the wicked were getting away with their sin but were exposed and appropriately punished.

   1.

   2.

   3.

EL ROI: "The God Who Sees" Genesis 16:13

> **Genesis 16:13**
> *Then she called the name of the LORD who spoke to her, "You are a God who sees"*

- Just as God saw the sufferings of Hagar in the desert, He sees you and will guide you out of the danger and trouble of your choices and circumstances. Revel in that and thank Him for seeing you.
- Praise God that He sees you and all that you are doing – both the evil and the good.
- Praise God that nothing that is being done in our day is hidden from the eyes of God: in politics, in church, in families, in companies. He sees it all and will bring our lives to account for what we have done.
- Praise God that I do not have to be noticed for what I have done to receive credit. God sees what I do and will reward me for my secret deeds of righteousness.

KANNA: "Jealous" (zealous) Exodus 20:5, 34:14

- God takes His relationship with you seriously to the point where He is willing to use the anthropomorphic terms of jealousy in regards to His love for you. He knows that your relationship with Him is vital to a full life. Therefore He wants you to value Him in His proper place as God and not as an add-on to your life.
- Give God praise for the strength of His love that it is possessive and concerned for our well being.
- Thank God for the times that His jealousy (kanna) has guided you away from other things that would have harmed you.

- If you have allowed anything to take first place in your heart other than God, remove it and return to your first love – the Lord Jesus Christ.

Exodus 20:5
You shall not worship them or serve them; for I, the LORD your God, am a jealous God, visiting the iniquity of the fathers on the children, on the third and the fourth generations of those who hate Me.

PALET: "Deliverer" Psalm 18:2

Psalm 18:2,3
The LORD is my rock and my fortress and my deliverer, My God, my rock, in whom I take refuge; My shield and the horn of my salvation, my stronghold.
I call upon the LORD, who is worthy to be praised, and I am saved from my enemies.

- Thank God for the fact that He always knows the way to escape and be safe from the difficulties and attacks that come your way.
- Thank God for at least three times that He has been your deliverer. These could be relationally, vocationally, personally, familial.

  1.

  2.

  3.

- If you are right now trying to deliver yourself, run into the arms of God and make sure that you let Him deliver you in His way.
- Thank Him for being your deliverer in times and ways that you do not know and may never know until heaven and you watch the tapes of your life from His perspective.

YESHA: (Y'shua) "Savior" Isaiah 43:3

Isaiah 43:3,4
For I am the LORD your God, The Holy One of Israel, your Savior...
Since you are precious in My sight, since you are honored and I love you...

- Thank God that He was willing to be your Savior.
- Give praise to God that He sought you out and drew you with His love so that He could save you.
- Thank God for saving you from three things

    1.

    2.

    3.

Day 23: Names: Gaol, Magen, Eyaluth, Tsaddiq, El-Olam

GAOL: "Redeemer" Job 19:25

> **Job 19:25**
> *As for me, I know that my Redeemer lives, and at the last He will take His stand on the earth.*

- Praise God that He has redeemed you from the punishment of your sins.
- Think about what your life would have been like without God and give thanks that He has redeemed.
- Right now God wants to redeem you from a number of things that are holding you back from enjoying His best. What are five of those things? Give thanks to God by faith for His redeeming you from them.

1.

2.

3.

4.

5.

MAGEN: "Shield" Psalm 3:3, 18:30

> **Psalm 3:3**
> *But You, O LORD, are a shield about me, my glory, and the One who lifts my head.*

- Praise God for being a shield around you.
- Praise God for all the temptations, difficulties, trouble, and evil from which He is presently shielding you.
- Whatever you are facing God wants to be your shield. Run into the protection of His name; live life His way and let Him wrap His shield around you. Trust Him for His shield about you and use it.

EYALUTH: "Strength" Psalm 22:19

Psalm 22:19
But You, O LORD, be not far off; O You my strength, hasten to my assistance.

- God is your strength – praise Him for His energy, power, and grace to do anything that He calls you to do.
- Praise God for the strength that is building within you to do His will in your present situation.
- Praise God for the strength that He has been in the past to accomplish His will.
- Praise God that He provides none of His strength to do sin and unrighteousness.

TSADDIQ: "Righteous One" Psalm 7:9

Psalm 7:9
O let the evil of the wicked come to an end, but establish the righteous; for the righteous God tries the hearts and minds.

- Praise God that He is righteous and not evil.
- Praise God that He is not deceptive and manipulative but instead righteous and upright.

- Give thanks to God that He is not the author or sponsor of evil.
- Magnify God for the fact that He always does what is right no matter how convoluted and/or sinful the situation.
- Give God praise that we do not have to doubt whether God will be righteous and pure. He will be. How wonderful that our great God does not turn, change, or hide a wicked aspect of Himself.
- Praise God that every attribute that He has will be expressed in righteousness – goodness, justice, omnipotence, omniscience, immutability, sovereignty, holiness, omnipresence, and truth.
- Praise God that was not He who twisted the wonder of creation into evil and selfishness but instead the devil and mankind.

EL-OLAM: "God of Everlasting Time" Genesis 21:33; Psalm 90:1-3

Psalm 90:1-6
A Prayer of Moses, the man of God. Lord, You have been our dwelling place in all generations. Before the mountains were born or You gave birth to the earth and the world, even from everlasting to everlasting, You are God. You turn man back into dust and say, "Return, O children of men." For a thousand years in Your sight are like yesterday when it passes by, or as a watch in the night. You have swept them away like a flood, they fall asleep; in the morning they are like grass which sprouts anew. In the morning it flourishes and sprouts anew; toward evening it fades and withers away.

- Praise God that He is outside of time.

- Praise God that He dwells in eternity.
- Praise God He sees and perceives the universe, earth, and mankind from outside of time.
- Praise God that He knows everything that will happen and could happen.
- Praise God that anything that is happening to you He knows how it happened how to work with it, how to turn it to good, and/or how to escape from it.

Day 24: Names: El-Gibhor, Zur, Sun of Righteousness, Attiq Yomim

EL-GIBHOR: "Mighty God" Isaiah 9:6

Isaiah 9:6
For a child will be born to us, a son will be given to us; And the government will rest on His shoulders; and His name will be called Wonderful Counselor, Mighty God, Eternal Father, Prince of Peace.

- Praise God that He is the Mighty God.
- Praise God that He is able to do whatever He pleases in Eternity and in the Universe.
- Praise God that His might is informed, directed, and controlled by all of the other perfections of His being.
- Praise God He has been mighty on your behalf.
- Give thanks for specific times that He has been Mighty on your behalf.
    - o From birth to 10 years of age
    - o From 11 to 20 years of age
    - o From 21 to 30 years of age
    - o From 31 to 40 years of age
    - o From 41 to 50 years of age
    - o From 51 to 60 years of age
    - o From 61 to 70 years of age
    - o From 71 to 80 years of age
    - o From 81 to 90 years of age
    - o From 91 to 100 years of age

ZUR: "God our Rock" Deuteronomy 32:18; Isaiah 30:29

> **Isaiah 30:29,30**
> *You will have songs as in the night when you keep the festival, and gladness of heart as when one marches to the sound of the flute, to go to the mountain of the LORD, to the Rock of Israel.*
> *And the LORD will cause His voice of authority to be heard, and the descending of His arm to be seen in fierce anger, and in the flame of a consuming fire in cloudburst, downpour and hailstones.*

- Praise God that He is the Rock that you can continually come for refuge, support, strength, and renewal
- Praise God that He is the Rock that will not change.
- Praise God that He has been your Rock where you could flee in times of trouble and pain.
- Remind yourself of the way that He has been your Rock in the past.

    1.

    2.

    3.

- How is God wanting to be your Rock right now? Act out your praise by letting Him be your Rock.

THE SUN OF RIGHTEOUSNESS (Malachi 4:2)

Malachi 4:2
But for you who fear My name, the sun of righteousness will rise with healing in its wings; and you will go forth and skip about like calves from the stall.

- Give thanks to God that He lights the way to righteous behavior.
- Exalt God that His righteousness does not change with passing of time – but what has been righteous will continue to be righteous.
- Praise God for the clarity of His righteousness. He has not left us to wonder what is righteous behavior and what is not.

Micah 6:8
He has told you, O man, what is good; and what does the LORD require of you but to do justice, to love kindness, And to walk humbly with your God?

- Praise God for the joy of living within His righteousness, His righteous boundaries, and having been given His righteousness as an undeserved gift through the life, death, and resurrection of His Son Jesus Christ.
- Praise God for the Ten Commandments' definition of love for God and love for others.

Thou shalt have no other god's before Me
Thou shalt not make for yourselves any graven images
Thou shalt not take the Name of the Lord your God in vain
Remember the Sabbath Day to keep it Holy
Honor your Father and your Mother
Thou shalt not murder
Thou shalt not commit adultery
Thou shalt not steal
Thou shalt not bear false witness against your neighbor
Thou shalt not covet anything that belongs to your neighbor

ATTIQ YOMIN: "Ancient of Days" Daniel 7:9

Daniel 7:9

"I kept looking until thrones were set up, and the Ancient of Days took His seat; His vesture was like white snow And the hair of His head like pure wool. His throne was ablaze with flames, its wheels were a burning fire.

A river of fire was flowing and coming out from before Him; thousands upon thousands were attending Him, and myriads upon myriads were standing before Him.

- Praise God that He is the Ancient of Days.
- Praise God that there has not been an animal, bacteria, fish, or bird that has lived upon the earth that God was not there for its beginning and ending.
- Praise God that no famous or infamous personage has ever lived that God was not there when they were born and when they died.
- Praise God that when time was invented, God was there inventing it.

- Praise God that all dimensionalities of time and space are understood by the Ancient of Days.
- Praise God that there is no secret knowledge or hidden agreements about the universe, earth, humanity, or your culture and/or community that God was not around to see and know all about it.
- Give God thanks that there is no being, no life force, nor entity that can claim to have been in existence before our God the Ancient of Days.

Day 25: Names: Melekh, Angel of the Lord, Father, First and Last

MELEKH: "King" Psalm 5:2, 29:10, 44:4, 47:6-8

Psalm 5:2
Heed the sound of my cry for help, my King and my God, For to You I pray.

Psalm 29:10
The LORD sat as King at the flood; yes, the LORD sits as King forever.

Psalm 47:6-9
Sing praises to God, sing praises; sing praises to our King, sing praises. For God is the King of all the earth; sing praises with a skillful psalm. God reigns over the nations, God sits on His holy throne. The princes of the people have assembled themselves as the people of the God of Abraham, for the shields of the earth belong to God; He is highly exalted.

- Praise God that He is King over all the nations.
- Praise God that no rebellion against His rules and laws will succeed.
- Give thanks that no matter how powerful a country or ruler becomes, He will not be able to throw off the rule of God forever.

THE ANGEL OF THE LORD: Genesis 16:7, 21:17; Exodus 3:6

Exodus 3:2-9
The angel of the LORD appeared to him in a blazing fire from the midst of a bush; and he looked, and behold, the bush was burning with fire, yet the bush was not consumed. So Moses said, "I must turn aside now and see this marvelous sight, why the bush is not burned up." When the LORD saw that he turned aside to look, God called to him from the midst of the bush and said, "Moses, Moses!" And he said, "Here I am." Then He said, "Do not come near here; remove your sandals from your feet, for the place on which you are standing is holy ground." He said also, "I am the God of your father, the God of Abraham, the God of Isaac, and the God of Jacob." Then Moses hid his face, for he was afraid to look at God. The LORD said, "I have surely seen the affliction of My people who are in Egypt, and have given heed to their cry because of their taskmasters, for I am aware of their sufferings. So I have come down to deliver them from the power of the Egyptians, and to bring them up from that land to a good and spacious land, to a land flowing with milk and honey, to the place of the Canaanite and the Hittite and the Amorite and the Perizzite and the Hivite and the Jebusite. Now, behold, the cry of the sons of Israel has come to Me; furthermore, I have seen the oppression with which the Egyptians are oppressing them."

- Most Christian scholars believe that the angel of the Lord is the Lord Jesus Christ appearing before His incarnation (birth by the Virgin Mary).

- Praise God that He personally seeks to communicate with those who will believe and follow Him.
- Praise God that God Himself is His own messenger.
- Praise God that we know that He sees the oppression of sinful men and sends help to change it.
- Praise God that He calls to you as He did to Moses from the burning bush.
- Praise God that He seeks out others to draw them into His love and embrace.

FATHER: Exodus 4:22-23; 2 Samuel 7:14-15

2 Samuel 7:14
I will be a father to him and he will be a son to Me; when he commits iniquity, I will correct him with the rod of men and the strokes of the sons of men.

- Praise God that He is a true father to us.
- Praise God that He comforts us like a father should.
- Praise God that he directs us like a father should.
- Praise God that He corrects us like a father should.
- Praise God that He disciplines us like a father should.
- Praise God that He does not wink at our actions which damage us or others but acts to stop them as a good father should.
- Praise God that He wants us as His child. He knows all about us but still wants to adopt us into His family.
- Praise God for how and when He has been a father to you.

1.

2.

3.

4.

5.

6.

7.

8.

9.

10.

THE FIRST AND LAST: Isaiah 44:6, 48:12

Isaiah 44:6
Thus says the LORD, the King of Israel and his Redeemer, the LORD of hosts: "I am the first and I am the last, and there is no God besides Me."

- Praise God that there were no gods or beings before Him and there will be no gods or beings after Him.
- Praise God that we are worshipping the Supreme God.
- Praise God that there will never be a time or circumstance when anyone will be able to say to our God, "You weren't at that meeting or those things were decided before you came on the scene."

Isaiah 48:12,13

Listen to Me, O Jacob, even Israel whom I called; I am He, I am the first, I am also the last. Surely My hand founded the earth, and My right hand spread out the heavens; when I call to them, they stand together.

• Praise God that He already knows how the world and the universe will end. He has already been there.

Day 26: Names: Kurios, Theos, Despotes, I am, Theotes

New Testament Names

KURIOS: "Lord"

Throughout Scripture -- both in the Old and New Testament -- God is called the Lord. In the Old Testament that word is Adonai. In the New Testament that word is Kurios. The meaning is essentially the same: the one who is the master and ruler.

- Praise God that He is master and ruler of the Universe.
- Praise God that He is the master and ruler of the angels.
- Praise God that He is the master and ruler of mankind.
- Praise God if He is your master and ruler.
- Give Him praise by admitting what areas in your life you are not allowing Him to have complete control and letting Him be Lord in those areas.

THEOS: "God"

The word THEOS is the Greek word for God that is untainted by the pantheon of Greek and Roman gods and goddess. This word stands for the God who is above, beyond, and before any so-called local gods. The New Testament never refers to God using the names of demi-gods of the culture at that time. This word in fact makes it clear that Christianity is referring to the God above all gods.

- Praise our great God for being God.
- Give thanks that He is the Supreme God above all gods and not a lesser being promoting or puffing Himself up.

- Give praise to God knowing that there will never be a time when another spiritual or human being will be able to rightly claim they are really the highest God.
- Marvel at the wonder of the God who is Supreme and yet wants a relationship with you – enough to send His only begotten Son to become human, live a perfect life, die as a sacrifice for your sins, and rise from the dead so that you could enjoy real relationship with the Supreme God.

DESPOTES: "Lord" Luke 2:29; Acts 4:24

The word despotes is the word for absolute Lord and master. We get our English word despot from it. It carries with it a measure of complete and total mastery. When Biblical characters use this word, they acknowledge the totalitarian nature of God's position of ruler of the world. It is an acknowledgement that God is God and there is no other and no power, direction, or authority that can even come close to His rulership.

> **Acts 4:24-28**
> *And when they heard this, they lifted their voices to God with one accord and said, "O Lord, it is You who MADE THE HEAVEN AND THE EARTH AND THE SEA, AND ALL THAT IS IN THEM, who by the Holy Spirit, through the mouth of our father David your servant, said, "WHY DID THE GENTILES RAGE, AND THE PEOPLES DEVISE FUTILE THINGS? „THE KINGS OF THE EARTH TOOK THEIR STAND, AND THE RULERS WERE GATHERED TOGETHER AGAINST THE LORD AND AGAINST HIS CHRIST."" For truly in this city there were gathered together against Your holy servant Jesus, whom You anointed, both Herod and Pontius Pilate, along with the Gentiles and the*

peoples of Israel, to do whatever Your hand and Your purpose predestined to occur.

- Praise God that He is the absolute lord over everything.
- Praise God that this role of absolute Lord was not given to or usurped by another.
- Praise God that the One who has despotic power and authority rules by the perfections of His nature, not His raw power.
- Give thanks to God that He has blocked many of the things that you thought would be best in your life. He is Lord.

"I AM": John 8:58. From the Hebrew Old Testament verb "to be" signifying a living, intelligent, personal being.

John 8:58

Jesus said to them, "Truly, truly, I say to you, before Abraham was born, I am." Therefore they picked up stones to throw at Him, but Jesus hid Himself and went out of the temple.

- Give thanks to God that Jesus is the ever-living God, who appeared to Moses in the burning bush.
- Praise God that Jesus is the self-existent One (along with the Father and the Spirit) whose possession of life itself requires that His name is the verb to be.
- Praise God that Jesus is "alive" in a way and at a level that we will never understand.
- Praise God that the Jews who were there at the time that Jesus makes the claim to be the great "I AM" did not miss the significance of His declaration and through their actions confirmed that Jesus was claiming to be God.
- Praise God that Jesus wants to fill you with His life and show you how to enjoy the life of God by being in relationship

with Him and living life His way with His values and His perspectives.

THEOTES: "Godhead" Colossians 2:9; Roman 1:20

The word Theotes is the word translated divine nature in the NASB translation of the Bible. It means the fullness of the deity, the Godhead in full trinity in a Christian understanding. It means that the personage being talked about is clearly God and with full nature of being God.

> ### Romans 1:20-23
> *For since the creation of the world His invisible attributes, His eternal power and divine nature, have been clearly seen, being understood through what has been made, so that they are without excuse. For even though they knew God, they did not honor Him as God or give thanks, but they became futile in their speculations, and their foolish heart was darkened. Professing to be wise, they became fools, and exchanged the glory of the incorruptible God for an image in the form of corruptible man and of birds and four-footed animals and crawling creatures.*

- Praise God that it is clear that He exists.
- Praise God that He has left numerous witnesses to Himself for everyone to follow and find if they would but look.
- Praise God that for those who respond to His drawing, He reveals Himself to be the One True God.
- Praise God that He drew you and that your turning aside to investigate (Exodus 3) allowed the scales to fall from your eyes and you to perceive the witnesses to His power that have been all around you.

- Praise God that you are no longer foolish in your speculations but instead enlightened because of His work in you and your honoring of Him in faith.
- Give thanks to God that you understand the purpose of life, the nature of Ultimate Reality, and are no longer lost in your particular selfishness and sins, because He revealed Himself, drew you, and you responded.

Day 27: Names: Soter, Jesus, Christ

SOTER: "Savior" Luke 1:47

> **Luke 1:47**
> *And Mary said: "My soul exalts the Lord, and my spirit has rejoiced in God my Savior. For He has had regard for the humble state of His bondslave; for behold, from this time on all generations will count me blessed. For the Mighty One has done great things for me; and holy is His name. AND HIS MERCY IS UPON GENERATION AFTER GENERATION TOWARD THOSE WHO FEAR HIM. He has done mighty deeds with His arm; He has scattered those who were proud in the thoughts of their heart. He has brought down rulers from their thrones, and has exalted those who were humble. HE HAS FILLED THE HUNGRY WITH GOOD THINGS; and sent away the rich empty-handed."*

- Praise God that He is the Savior.
- Give thanks to God that He did not hit the reset button and discard this whole world and its sinfulness, but instead He is the Savior who redeems that which is hopelessly broken and dysfunctional.
- Bless God for His saving of you.
- Remind God and yourself of at least five ways that He has saved you.

   1.

   2.

3.

4.

5.

JESUS: From the Hebrew "Joshua" meaning JEHOVAH (Yahweh) IS SALVATION.

Matthew 1:19-21

And Joseph her husband, being a righteous man and not wanting to disgrace her, planned to send her away secretly. But when he had considered this, behold, an angel of the Lord appeared to him in a dream, saying, "Joseph, son of David, do not be afraid to take Mary as your wife; for the Child who has been conceived in her is of the Holy Spirit. She will bear a Son; and you shall call His name Jesus, for He will save His people from their sins."

- Praise God that He sent His only begotten Son to save us when were unworthy of salvation.
- Praise God that Jesus' rescue mission did not fail but instead resulted in the rescue of millions of people from the punishment of their own sins.
- Praise God that Jesus was real – born to a real mother, a heavenly Father. He lived a real life and laid His life down on a real hill called Golgotha.
- Praise God that you have been saved from the penalty of your sins if you believe in Jesus as your Savior.
- Praise God that you are being saved from the power of sin in your present life as you continue to trust Christ and learn His way of life.

- Praise God that you will be saved from the presence of sin when His salvation of you is complete in heaven.
- Give thanks to Jesus for enduring the shame and humbling Himself to the point of death on a cross so that He would enjoy fellowship with those who believed in Him.
- Give Jesus praise for being the Savior of the World.
- Give thanks to Jesus for His work by choosing to believe in Him as your Savior if you have never done that before.

CHRIST: is equivalent to the Hebrew 'Messiah' (Meshiach), "The Anointed One"

Matthew 16:13-16
Now when Jesus came into the district of Caesarea Philippi, He was asking His disciples, "Who do people say that the Son of Man is?" And they said, "Some say John the Baptist; and others, Elijah; but still others, Jeremiah, or one of the prophets." He said to them, "But who do you say that I am?" Simon Peter answered, "You are the Christ, the Son of the living God."

- Praise God that He sent an Anointed One; long predicted and finally sent.
- Give thanks to God that the Messiah is Jesus.
- Praise God that while the Jews missed their Messiah, He offered Himself to the Gentiles.
- Give thanks to God by telling God again that you need a Messiah, an Anointed One, to rescue you.

Day 28: Names: Shepherd of the Sheep, Master, King of Kings, Lord of Lords

Other New Testament Titles for Jesus

Give praise to the Lord Jesus that He successfully fulfilled His mission of redemption.

Ask Him to open your eyes to see the various aspects of who He is, what He does, and who He wants to be to you.

Ask Him to be in your life the various roles that are suggested by the titles that He takes. Yield to Christ in these various roles and ministries in your life.

SHEPHERD OF THE SHEEP: Hebrews 13:20

> **Hebrews 13:20**
> *Now the God of peace, who brought up from the dead the great Shepherd of the sheep through the blood of the eternal covenant, even Jesus our Lord.*

- Praise God that the Savior is one who shepherds the people that believe and follow Him. He is not a task oriented being that accomplishes the mission but does not deal with the people who are then saved.
- Praise God that His shepherding is active and not passive. Like a good shepherd He will follow the wayward sheep, discipline it to turn it back, and even throw it over His shoulders to keep it from going too far off track.

- Praise God that He shepherds you at crucial times in your life. List five to remind yourself.

  1.

  2.

  3.

  4.

  5.

- Give God thanks for the fact that He wants to shepherd you right now in the midst of the problems, situations, and opportunities that you are presently experiencing.

MASTER

2 Timothy 2:21
Therefore, if anyone cleanses himself from these things, he will be a vessel for honor, sanctified, useful to the Master, prepared for every good work.

- Praise God that He is the rightful Master of every life on the planet.
- Praise God that you have seen the error of your arrogant ways and have made Jesus the Master of your life. If you have not, then do so now. If it has been a while since you truly followed the one that is the rightful Master, then surrender and exalt the Name of Jesus by giving Him the rightful place as Master.

KING OF KINGS

1 Timothy 6:15

He who is the blessed and only Sovereign, the King of kings and Lord of lords.

- Praise God that He is above every earthly or supernatural ruler ever.
- Marvel at the authority of God to be over every ruler.
- Mention five names of rulers at present or in history and state out loud that God is the authority over those authorities and leaders.

Revelation 17:14

These will wage war against the Lamb, and the Lamb will overcome them, because He is Lord of lords and King of kings, and those who are with Him are the called and chosen and faithful.

- Realize that there will always be leaders, rulers, and spirits that will strive to set themselves up against or above God, but God will make a show of them and assert His rightful place as King of Kings.
- Thank God that He is the rightful ruler of your life, not the phony authorities who wounded or hurt you.
- Praise God for being a compassionate King of Kings and not a despotic ruler.

LORD OF LORDS

Revelation 19:11-16

And I saw heaven opened, and behold, a white horse, and He who sat on it is called Faithful and True, and in righteousness He judges and wages war. His eyes are a flame of fire, and on His head are many diadems; and He has a name written on Him which no one knows except Himself. He is clothed with a robe dipped in blood, and His name is called The Word of God. And the armies which are in heaven, clothed in fine linen, white and clean, were following Him on white horses. From His mouth comes a sharp sword, so that with it He may strike down the nations, and He will rule them with a rod of iron; and He treads the wine press of the fierce wrath of God, the Almighty. And on His robe and on His thigh He has a name written, "KING OF KINGS, AND LORD OF LORDS."

•   Praise God that there will come a day when the heavens will open and Jesus the Christ will come to assert His right to rule.

Day 29: Names: Bishop and Guardian of our Souls, Deliverer, Adocate

BISHOP AND GUARDIAN OF OUR SOULS

1 Peter 2:25

For you were continually straying like sheep, but now you have returned to the Shepherd and Guardian of your souls.

- Praise God that He takes the responsibility to watch over our souls and guard them.
- Give God thanks for the times when He has protected you from things you wanted to do by not answering your prayers.
- Give thanks to God for all the ways that He has tried to discourage you from going down a path that He knew would be destructive to you.
- Praise God by returning to the Shepherd and Guardian of your souls by admitting that you have done a lousy job of running your own life every time you resisted His direction and instead done things your way.

DELIVERER

Romans 11:26

and so all Israel will be saved; just as it is written, "THE DELIVERER WILL COME FROM ZION, HE WILL REMOVE UNGODLINESS FROM JACOB."

- We are so corrupted that we do not think of being delivered from the ungodliness all around us; but praise God, Jesus will come deliver us not just from the penalty of sin but also from the presence of sin, ungodliness, and wickedness.

• What types of temptations and ungodliness is Jesus trying to deliver you from and you are resisting? Praise God by letting Him do this vital function of removing you from the corruption that is all around you.

ADVOCATE

1 John 2:1,2
My little children, I am writing these things to you so that you may not sin. And if anyone sins, we have an Advocate with the Father, Jesus Christ the righteous; and He Himself is the propitiation for our sins; and not for ours only, but also for those of the whole world.

• Give God praise and thanks that when the devil accuses us and slanders us, we have a divine advocate so that none of the schemes of the devil will succeed.
• Praise God that Jesus pleads for us and argues for us in the heavenly places.
• Praise God that Jesus is the only human who is perfectly righteous and able to be in the presence of the Father. It is His perfections of righteousness that He offers on our behalf – even though we do not deserve them.
• Praise God that when you will most need a defense lawyer – when you appear before the throne of the Almighty God on judgment day – you have the best one ever: Jesus Christ the Righteous.
• Praise God that Jesus is the full answer to the wrath of God for your selfishness and sin and the selfishness and sin of the whole world.

- Praise God that forgiveness through Jesus' gift is available to everyone who will believe.

Hebrews 7:25
Therefore He is able also to save forever those who draw near to God through Him, since He always lives to make intercession for them.

- Praise God that Jesus is our Advocate right now against the accusations of the evil one in the heavens and in our minds.

Day 30: Names: Second Adam, Chief Cornerstone

SECOND ADAM

Romans 5:12, 14, 15

Therefore, just as through one man sin entered into the world, and death through sin, and so death spread to all men, because all sinned— Nevertheless death reigned from Adam until Moses, even over those who had not sinned in the likeness of the offense of Adam, who is a type of Him who was to come. But the free gift is not like the transgression. For if by the transgression of the one the many died, much more did the grace of God and the gift by the grace of the one Man, Jesus Christ, abound to the many.

- Praise God that Jesus was willing to become human, live the perfect human life, and then willingly give up that life so that many could be blessed through His righteousness.
- Give thanks to God that you do not have to sin and do not have to let sin dictate how you live your life.
- Praise God that there is no limit to the power of the gift; it extends to as many as will receive Him.

CHIEF CORNERSTONE

Ephesians 2:20-23

...having been built on the foundation of the apostles and prophets, Christ Jesus Himself being the corner stone, in whom the whole building, being fitted together, is growing into a holy temple in the

*Lord, in whom you also are being built together into
a dwelling of God in the Spirit.*

- Praise God that He is building a living Holy Temple where the God in Trinity will dwell, and we are the building materials of the walls and Jesus is the cornerstone.
- Give thanks to God that He reached out to us who were far from God and drew us near through Jesus who is the cornerstone of the project He is building through history.
- Give thanks to God that down through the history of the Christian church, God continues to add to the building those who will believe in His cornerstone. One day in heaven we will be able to catch a glimpse of its splendor.

Day 31: Names: Immanuel, First Born, Head of the Body, Physician

IMMANUEL

Matthew 1:23
BEHOLD, THE VIRGIN SHALL BE WITH CHILD AND SHALL BEAR A SON, AND THEY SHALL CALL HIS NAME IMMANUEL, which translated means, "GOD WITH US."

- Praise God that He has not left us on this space ship called earth to fend for ourselves but has come to be with us in the presence of His Son, Jesus the Christ.
- Praise God that He will one day tabernacle with us constantly in heaven. This is an amazing promise to be reveled in constantly before it happens and then embraced in when it happens.

Revelation 21:3-5
And I heard a loud voice from the throne, saying, "Behold, the tabernacle of God is among men, and He will dwell among them, and they shall be His people, and God Himself will be among them, and He will wipe away every tear from their eyes; and there will no longer be any death; there will no longer be any mourning, or crying, or pain; the first things have passed away."

- Give thanks to God that even though He has physically left us, He has not left us at all.

John 14:16-19
I will ask the Father, and He will give you another Helper, that He may be with you forever; that is the Spirit of truth, whom the world cannot receive, because it does not see Him or know Him, but you know Him because He abides with you and will be in you. I will not leave you as orphans; I will come to you. After a little while the world will no longer see Me, but you will see Me.

*   Give thanks to God that He came and that He ascended to Heaven so that He could send the Spirit of Christ to dwell with all of us.

John 16:5-7
But I tell you the truth, it is to your advantage that I go away; for if I do not go away, the Helper will not come to you; but if I go, I will send Him to you.

FIRST BORN

Revelation 1:5
...and from Jesus Christ, the faithful witness, the firstborn of the dead, and the ruler of the kings of the earth. To Him who loves us and released us from our sins by His blood.

*   Praise God that He is not asking us to trust Him for a process after death that He has not Himself personally gone through in the person of Jesus.
*   Praise God that Jesus is the first born of the dead having conquered the grave through the power of God coursing through His humanity.

- Give thanks that Jesus was the first to die and receives both the title and leadership of those who would approach God through His righteousness, but He will not be the last. He has opened a way to God through His perfect life, death, and resurrection that millions will go through into a deep intimate relationship with God.

HEAD OF THE BODY

Colossians 1:18
He is also head of the body, the church; and He is the beginning, the firstborn from the dead, so that He Himself will come to have first place in everything.

- Praise God that Jesus has not abandoned His congregations to fend for themselves, but He is the active head of the body of Christ, the church.
- Give thanks to Christ for His active leadership of the church by spending time listening to His leadership and doing what He wants the church to do.
- Give praise to God by answering and acting on the answers to this question, "If God had free reign in this church what would He do with worship, evangelism, fellowship, discipleship, and service/compassion."

PHYSICIAN

Luke 4:23
And He said to them, "No doubt you will quote this proverb to Me, 'Physician, heal yourself! Whatever we heard was done at Capernaum, do here in your hometown as well.'"
- Praise God that He is the Great Physician.
- Praise God that He can heal any sickness and any disease.

- Praise God that He knows what is the true source of the sickness.
- Praise God that He wants health and wholeness in our soul and spirit even more than our bodies.

Day 32: Names: Rock, Root of Jesse, Stone, Chief Apostle

ROCK

Matthew 16:18
I also say to you that you are Peter, and upon this rock I will build My church; and the gates of Hades will not overpower it.

- Praise God that Christianity is not built on some flimsy stories but the Rock which is Jesus Christ – His birth, life, death, and resurrection.
- Praise God that our Rock is stronger than the attacks of the enemy that seek to destroy Him. Christ's church has existed for over 2,000 years and will continue until He comes again.

I Corinthians 10:4
And all drank the same spiritual drink, for they were drinking from a spiritual rock which followed them; and the rock was Christ.

- Praise God that Christ is our Rock who provides us with spiritual nourishment for the long journey to Him.
- Praise God for the pictures of Christ in the Old Testament and specifically in the story of the Exodus.

ROOT OF JESSE

Romans 15:12
Again Isaiah says, "THERE SHALL COME THE ROOT OF JESSE, AND HE WHO ARISES TO

RULE OVER THE GENTILES, IN HIM SHALL THE GENTILES HOPE."

- Praise God that just as He predicted 1,000 years before Christ, one of David's descendants rose up and asserts His rulership over the whole world – Jesus Christ the Righteous, the Son of David, the root of Jesse.
- Praise God that Jesus is historically the root of Jesse and the Son of David.

STONE

Romans 9:33
just as it is written, "BEHOLD, I LAY IN ZION A STONE OF STUMBLING AND A ROCK OF OFFENSE, AND HE WHO BELIEVES IN HIM WILL NOT BE DISAPPOINTED."

- Praise God that a person must humble himself to accept help from Christ.
- Praise God that a person must accept the offense that they are not good enough to earn their way into heaven and must accept God's help through Christ.
- Praise God that many who have stumbled over Jesus of Nazareth have come to believe in Him and not be disappointed.

Ephesians 2:20
...having been built on the foundation of the apostles and prophets, Christ Jesus Himself being the corner stone.

- Praise God that while few of the religious experts of Jesus' day accepted Him as the foundation for building the true path to God – but God accepted Him as the chief corner stone for the only true way to God.

- Praise and exalt God by building upon the foundation of Christ and the apostles through good works and righteous living.

CHIEF APOSTLE

Hebrews 3:1
Therefore, holy brethren, partakers of a heavenly calling, consider Jesus, the Apostle and High Priest of our confession.

- Praise God that Jesus is the leader of all Christians and the one who was sent from heaven to earth with a mission to accomplish and He accomplished it – the redemption of mankind.

Day 33: Names: Great High Priest, Author and Perfecter of our Faith

GREAT HIGH PRIEST

Hebrews 4:14
Therefore, since we have a great high priest who has passed through the heavens, Jesus the Son of God, let us hold fast our confession.

- Praise God that Jesus is a true High Priest who can take our confession of faith in Him and our own sinfulness to the actual altar in heaven.
- Praise God that He can listen to our sins and have a solution to them: His own sacrifice.
- Praise God that He is able to minister to us in the midst of our mistakes, selfishness, and sins because He has no ministry to Himself in this regard.

PIONEER AND PERFECTER OF OUR FAITH
OR AUTHOR AND FINISHER

Hebrews 12:2
...fixing our eyes on Jesus, the author and perfecter of faith, who for the joy set before Him endured the cross, despising the shame, and has sat down at the right hand of the throne of God.

- Praise God that He originated the idea of faith as the way of salvation and relationship with God.
- Praise God for the wisdom of His pathway of faith as it eliminates all pride and self-generated righteousness.

- Praise God that He completed the way of faith so that it would work – even though the completing cost Him His life.
- Praise God that He supplies you with the faith that is needed for you to complete the journey of faith laid out for you.
- Praise God that the way of faith is always the way to connect with God throughout the Christian life.
- Praise God for believing Him today about that element of His will that you have been hesitating – but are truly clear that it is His will.

Day 34: Names: Lamb of God, Lamb Slain Before the Foundation of the World, Lord God Almighty, Logos, Sophia

LAMB OF GOD

John 1:29
The next day he saw Jesus coming to him and said, "Behold, the Lamb of God who takes away the sin of the world!"

- There was never any question why God the Son became a man. It was to be the sacrificial lamb for the sins of the world. Praise God that He was willing to take on this assignment and carry it out to its completion.
- Praise God that He took your sins on Himself and paid for the penalty that should have been yours.

LAMB SLAIN BEFORE THE FOUNDATION OF THE WORLD

1 Peter 1:17-21
If you address as Father the One who impartially judges according to each one"s work, conduct yourselves in fear during the time of your stay on earth; knowing that you were not redeemed with perishable things like silver or gold from your futile way of life inherited from your forefathers, but with precious blood, __as of a lamb unblemished and spotless, the blood of Christ. For He was foreknown before the foundation of the world__, but has appeared in these last times for the sake of you who through Him are believers in God, who raised

*Him from the dead and gave Him glory, so that your
faith and hope are in God.*

- Give thanks to God that from before the time that the Universe was created and set into motion, He knew that humanity would choose against Him and need to be redeemed. And that in His plan, He knew that He would need to sacrifice His only begotten Son to buy out of the slave market of sin the humanity He did not need to create.
- Praise God that there is never a part of the timeline of our Universe that God does not know everything about – from its going wrong to what is needed to set it right.
- Praise God that for every time you go off track from His will, He knows what it will take to bring you back to living in His grace; and that every straying that you do was what required Him to sacrifice His Son.
- Praise God that when He thought out all that would be required to redeem mankind from the depths of wickedness and selfishness that would infect every person, He still chose to create even though He knew the price would be high for Him personally. If He had not, you and I would be here.

LORD GOD ALMIGHTY

Revelation 21:22
*I saw no temple in it, for the Lord God the Almighty
and the Lamb are its temple.*

- Praise God that in heaven we will have immediate and direct access to the Tri-une God.
- Praise God that in heaven we will constantly be aware of the sacrifice that Jesus the Christ made for us so that we can be inside the celestial city.

- Praise God that there will never be a question who the authority or leader of heaven is. There will be no hint of rebellion in the presence of the Lord God the Almighty.

LOGOS

John 1:1-5,14

In the beginning was the Word, and the Word was with God, and the Word was God. He was in the beginning with God. All things came into being through Him, and apart from Him nothing came into being that has come into being. In Him was life, and the life was the Light of men. The Light shines in the darkness, and the darkness did not comprehend it.
And the Word became flesh, and dwelt among us, and we saw His glory, glory as of the only begotten from the Father, full of grace and truth.

- Exalt Jesus for being the Living Word of God, for being with God in the beginning of space and time and matter, and for being God Himself.
- Praise Jesus for creating the Universe and all the laws that govern it and in this way helping us understand more of the attributes and thoughts of God.
- Praise God that there was never a time before the Son existed, but He has always existed as a personal being – the perfected expression of God.

Hebrews 1:1-3

God, after He spoke long ago to the fathers in the prophets in many portions and in many ways, in these last days has spoken to us in His Son, whom He appointed heir of all things, through whom also He made the world. And He is the radiance of His glory and the exact representation of His nature, and upholds all things by the word of His power. When He had made purification of sins, He sat down at the right hand of the Majesty on high.

- Praise God that He is incomprehensible. He will always have aspects of His being, nature, and actions that we do not understand. He is the infinite God beyond understanding and beyond expressing to any being less than Himself.
- But praise God that He has expressed Himself truly to us in Jesus of Nazareth, the God-man. When we see what Jesus does, we are watching what God is and does.
- Watching Jesus is as close to understanding the nature, thoughts, and actions of God as we will ever get on this planet. The Living Word is the expression of God, and we comprehend so very little of it. But we do truly comprehend some of who He is. Give Him praise for trying to communicate with us such limited creatures.

Revelation 19:11-13
And I saw heaven opened, and behold, a white horse, and He who sat on it is called Faithful and True, and in righteousness He judges and wages war. His eyes are a flame of fire, and on His head are many diadems; and He has a name written on Him which no one knows except Himself. He is clothed with a robe dipped in blood, and His name is called The Word of God.

- Praise God that there will come a time when the Living Word of God will strip away the false realities of our world's systems and display the reality that there is one True God and that all other versions of reality are deceptive and destructive.

- Praise God that the Living Word will speak and set the world right with the true expression of God. He will make the reality of the world systems and cultures match the ultimate reality of heaven and earth.

SOPHIA

Colossians 2:2,3
...that their hearts may be encouraged, having been knit together in love, and attaining to all the wealth that comes from the full assurance of understanding, resulting in a true knowledge of God"s mystery, that is, Christ Himself, in whom are hidden all the treasures of wisdom and knowledge.

- Praise God that Jesus is full of wisdom and knowledge and not just the temporary carrier of the Spirit of God.
- Praise God that Jesus is Himself the mystery of God and the key to understanding the work of God.
- Praise Jesus the Christ who has all the answers to the questions that we have been longing to ask.

Day 35: Names: Counselor, Comforter, Baptizer, Strengthener, Sanctifier, Spirit of Christ

NAMES FOR THE HOLY SPIRIT

- Give praise to the Holy Spirit that He ministers to us in all these various roles and ministries:

    Counselor, Comforter, Baptizer, Strengthener, Sanctifier, Spirit of Christ, Spirit of the Lord, Spirit of Wisdom, Spirit of Understanding, Spirit of Counsel, Spirit of Strength, Spirit of Knowledge, Spirit of the Fear of the Lord, Spirit of Holiness.

- Ask Him to open your eyes to see these operating in, to, and for you, that you might adequately thank Him.
- Ask Him to be and Yield to Him in these various roles and ministries in your life.

COUNSELOR

John 14:26
But the Helper, the Holy Spirit, whom the Father will send in My name, He will teach you all things, and bring to your remembrance all that I said to you.

- Give God praise for giving us the Holy Spirit who helps us, counsels us, and guides us.
- Praise God by listening to the guidance of the Holy Spirit and doing what is righteous.

Isaiah 30:21
Your ears will hear a word behind you, "This is the way, walk in it," whenever you turn to the right or to the left.

- Give God joy and delight in you by doing as He prompts.
- Give thanks to God for the ways that He has guided and led you in the past. Thank Him for five specific times.

1.

2.

3.

4.

5.

Ephesians 4:30
Do not grieve the Holy Spirit of God, by whom you were sealed for the day of redemption.

COMFORTER

John 14:16
I will ask the Father, and He will give you another Helper (comforter, encourager), that He may be with you forever.

- The Holy Spirit is right now comforting you in a number of ways – be grateful for three of those ways.

1.

2.

3.

- The Holy Spirit has been your comforter. Remind yourself of how He has comforted you in this last year.

  1.

  2.

  3.

  4.

  5.

2 Corinthians 1:3,4

Blessed be the God and Father of our Lord Jesus Christ, the Father of mercies and God of all comfort, who comforts us in all our affliction so that we will be able to comfort those who are in any affliction with the comfort with which we ourselves are comforted by God.

- It is important that we realize that God does not comfort us by necessarily taking the pain or problem away. He comforts us in the midst of our trials. He sends comfort through others.
- Give God thanks that you have been sustained or are being sustained through a difficult time.
- Let God know that you are willing to share with others what God has taught you, so that you can comfort them.

BAPTIZER

1 Corinthians 12:13
For by one Spirit we were all baptized into one body, whether Jews or Greeks, whether slaves or free, and we were all made to drink of one Spirit.

- Give thanks to God that He has given you His Holy Spirit if you are a Christian.
- Praise God that His Holy Spirit has made you a part of a new forever family called the family of God.
- Praise God that irrespective of status in this present world, the Holy Spirit connects us to God's family.
- Praise God and drink deeply of the Holy Spirit letting His wisdom, guidance, knowledge, and love fill your life.

STRENGTHENER

1 Timothy 1:12
But the Lord is faithful, and He will strengthen and protect you from the evil one.

- Praise God that He will strengthen us when we need Him.

2 Timothy 4:17
But the Lord stood with me and strengthened me, so that through me the proclamation might be fully accomplished, and that all the Gentiles might hear; and I was rescued out of the lion"s mouth.

- Praise God that He has strengthened us in the past. Remind yourself of three times you were in need of His strength and what He did to supply strength to you.

1.

2.

3.

2 Thessalonians 3:3
*I thank Christ Jesus our Lord, who has strengthened
me, because He considered me faithful, putting me
into service.*

• Praise God that He is right now sending you the strength
  you need to endure and succeed. Look around you and
  notice the ways He is sending His strength and thank Him.

1.

2.

3.

4.

5.

SANCTIFIER

1 Peter 1:2
*...according to the foreknowledge of God the Father,
by the sanctifying work of the Spirit, to obey Jesus
Christ and be sprinkled with His blood: May grace
and peace be yours in the fullest measure.*

• Praise God that the Holy Spirit is working in us and with us
  to set us apart from those who are not believers.

- Praise God that the Holy Spirit is working both positively and negatively to make us set apart for our intended purpose.
- Give thanks to God by letting Him set you apart and no longer avoiding the positive things He wants you to do and saying no to the negative things that He wants you to give up.
- Remind yourself of the progress that the Holy Spirit has made already in your life. What have you said yes to that has set you apart?

    1.

    2.

    3.

- What have you said no to that has set you apart for God's purposes?

    1.

    2.

    3.

SPIRIT OF CHRIST

Romans 8:9

However, you are not in the flesh but in the Spirit, if indeed the Spirit of God dwells in you. But if anyone does not have the Spirit of Christ, he does not belong to Him.

- Thank God that the Spirit of Christ is in you, directing you, and ministering to you.

- Praise God for the still small voice of the Spirit of Christ inside you, leading you away from temptation and selfishness and directing you toward love, humility, and justice.
- Remind yourself of His direction of you in the last year and praise Him for those promptings.

1.

2.

3.

1 Peter 1:10,11
As to this salvation, the prophets who prophesied of the grace that would come to you made careful searches and inquiries, seeking to know what person or time the Spirit of Christ within them was indicating as He predicted the sufferings of Christ and the glories to follow.

- Praise God that the same Spirit of Christ that operated in the prophets of old operates in you to move you to holiness.
- Thank God that you live in the time when Christ is known and the wonder of His sacrifice and person are open information.
- Give thanks to God that the second coming of Christ is as sure as the first coming has proved to be.

Philippians 1:19
For I know that this will turn out for my deliverance through your prayers and the provision of the Spirit of Jesus Christ.

- Thank God that He listens to the prayers of His believers to provide strength, provision, and deliverance to us.
- Praise God that in knowing the future He can have provisions waiting for us at just the right time in just the right place.
- Thank Him for His provision for you in the past.

1.

2.

3.

4.

5.

Day 36: Names: The Seven-fold Spirit: Spirit of the Lord, Wisdom, Understanding, Counsel, Strength, Knowledge, Fear of the Lord, Spirit of Holiness

SEVEN-FOLD SPIRIT

Isaiah 11:1-3
Then a shoot will spring from the stem of Jesse, and a branch from his roots will bear fruit. The Spirit of the LORD will rest on Him, the spirit of wisdom and understanding, the spirit of counsel and strength, the spirit of knowledge and the fear of the LORD. And He will delight in the fear of the LORD, and He will not judge by what His eyes see, nor make a decision by what His ears hear.

SPIRIT OF THE LORD

- Praise God that the Holy Spirit has authority and power to execute the will of God.
- Praise God that He gives that authority and power to believers to accomplish His will for their lives.

SPIRIT OF WISDOM

- Praise God that the Holy Spirit is full of wisdom.
- Praise God that He always knows the way to have God win, others win, and the individual win while allowing the wicked to lose.

SPIRIT OF UNDERSTANDING

- Praise God that the Holy Spirit understands all the connections between things.
- Give thanks to God that He shares His understanding of those connections with those who listen hard at His truth recorded in the Scriptures.

SPIRIT OF COUNSEL

- Praise God that the Holy Spirit is full of specific personal advice for particular problems.
- Praise God that there is never a situation you can face where God would say, "Well, I have never heard of that and don't know what to do."
- He always knows what to do and say – give thanks to Him that He is never stumped. The only question is whether people will do what He says.

SPIRIT OF STRENGTH

- Praise God that He never runs out of strength.
- Praise God that He is willing to share His strength with those who wait upon Him. Waiting on the Lord is same as delighting in Him and is what you are doing when you are praising Him.

SPIRIT OF KNOWLEDGE

- Praise God that the Holy Spirit knows everything there is to know. There are no facts that escape His notice. There is no information that He does not know.
- Praise God that He can communicate what we need to know – when we need to know it.

SPIRIT OF FEAR OF THE LORD

- Praise God that the Holy Spirit is the spirit of reverence and awe for the person of God.
- Praise God that we experience this aspect of the Holy Spirit when we praise God.

THE SPIRIT OF HOLINESS

Romans 1:4

...who was declared the Son of God with power by the resurrection from the dead, according to the Spirit of holiness, Jesus Christ our Lord.

- Praise God that the Holy Spirit is Holy and not deceptive, manipulative, or wicked.
- Praise God that He is pure and above sin.
- Praise God that holiness and order are His nature not chaos, disorder, and destruction.

Day 37: Works: Creation

Works

- There are four dominant works of God that radiate His glory and demand our praise. These four acts of God are regularly and constantly referred to in Scripture: These are His Creation, the Exodus, Salvation, and the Scriptures.

Creation Genesis 1:1; Psalm 19:1

Psalm 19:1
The heavens are telling of the glory of God; and their expanse is declaring the work of His hands. Day to day pours forth speech, and night to night reveals knowledge. There is no speech, nor are there words; their voice is not heard. Their line has gone out through all the earth, and their utterances to the end of the world. In them He has placed a tent for the sun, which is as a bridegroom coming out of his chamber; it rejoices as a strong man to run his course. Its rising is from one end of the heavens, and its circuit to the other end of them; and there is nothing hidden from its heat.

- Adore God for His creation. Tell Him of your awe and joy in seeing and experiencing various parts of His creation.
- Give thanks to God for everything in His creation from the laws that govern His creation to the creatures that inhabit it.
- Adore God for His power, wisdom, knowledge, and goodness shown in the creation.

Romans 1:20

For since the creation of the world His invisible attributes, His eternal power and divine nature, have been clearly seen, being understood through what has been made, so that they are without excuse.

• Thank Him for five specific things in the universe.

1.

2.

3.

4.

5.

Day 38: Works: Exodus

Exodus: 1 Corinthians 10:1-12

- As the ancient world was rebelling and running away from an accurate knowledge of God, He chose an insignificant man to start a whole new race who would preserve the true knowledge of God for the whole world.
- Praise God for His choice of Abram.
- Praise God for His preservation of the Jewish nation inspite of their own rebellion and disobedience to God.

1 Corinthians 10:1-12

For I do not want you to be unaware, brethren, that our fathers were all under the cloud and all passed through the sea; and all were baptized into Moses in the cloud and in the sea; and all ate the same spiritual food; and all drank the same spiritual drink, for they were drinking from a spiritual rock which followed them; and the rock was Christ. Nevertheless, with most of them God was not well-pleased; for they were laid low in the wilderness. Now these things happened as examples for us, so that we would not crave evil things as they also craved. Do not be idolaters, as some of them were; as it is written, "THE PEOPLE SAT DOWN TO EAT AND DRINK, AND STOOD UP TO PLAY." Nor let us act immorally, as some of them did, and twenty-three thousand fell in one day. Nor let us try the Lord, as some of them did, and were destroyed by the serpents. Nor grumble, as some of them did, and were destroyed by the destroyer. Now these things happened to them as an example, and they

were written for our instruction, upon whom the
ends of the ages have come. Therefore let him who
thinks he stands take heed that he does not fall.

- Thank God for displaying His power and His care in the Exodus.
- Thank God for preserving the knowledge of Himself.
- Thank Him that He will also rescue you.
- Thank Him for the examples in the Exodus – both good and bad.

Day 39: Works: Salvation

Salvation: Ephesians 3:17

- Thank Him for doing all the work, planning, and accomplishing salvation for rebellious humanity

Romans 8:29-35
For those whom He foreknew, He also predestined to become conformed to the image of His Son, so that He would be the firstborn among many brethren; and these whom He predestined, He also called; and these whom He called, He also justified; and these whom He justified, He also glorified. What then shall we say to these things? If God is for us, who is against us? He who did not spare His own Son, but delivered Him over for us all, how will He not also with Him freely give us all things? Who will bring a charge against God"s elect? God is the one who justifies; who is the one who condemns? Christ Jesus is He who died, yes, rather who was raised, who is at the right hand of God, who also intercedes for us. Who will separate us from the love of Christ? Will tribulation, or distress, or persecution, or famine, or nakedness, or peril, or sword?

- Give God praise for all the aspects of your salvation.
- **Foreknowledge:** He knew you before you were born.
- **Election:** He chose you before the foundation of the world.
- **Restraining ministry of Holy Spirit:** The Holy Spirit held you back from all the sin you were capable of and your society from all the evil it was capable of.

- **Conviction ministry of Holy Spirit:** The Holy Spirit brought conviction to your heart that you were a sinner and needed God.
- **God's call:** God drew you to Himself.
- **Faith:** You trusted in Christ to be your way to heaven and relationship with God.
- **Conversion:** He converted you from a child of darkness following vain reasonings to a child of light guided into by His truth and His love.
- **Spirit Baptism:** His Holy Spirit baptized you into the body of Christ making you a part of His forever family.
- **Indwelling of the Holy Spirit:** His Holy Spirit came to dwell in you.
- **Justification:** You were declared righteous before God because of the life and death of Christ on your behalf.
- **Regeneration:** God gave you life, spiritual connection to Him, and a new nature.
- **Union with Christ:** You were united with Jesus in His life, death, and resurrection.
- **Adoption:** You were adopted into God's family as a heir of life.
- **Sealing of the Holy Spirit:** You were sealed with the Holy Spirit bound for heaven.
- **Sanctification:** You are being set apart for God's intended purpose for you to glorify Him.
- **Filling of the Holy Spirit:** The Holy Spirit seeks to fill you to overflowing with Himself that you would produce the fruit of the Spirit in every arena of your life.
- **Spiritual Gifts:** The Holy Spirit gave you a gift(s) to build up the church – His body.
- **Glorification:** The Lord finishes the job of salvation by perfecting you in heaven.
- **Redemption of the body:** The Lord resurrects your body and perfects it, also making it a heavenly dwelling.

- **Marriage Supper of the Lamb:** Believers are invited to a feast celebrating the victory of the Lord Jesus Christ with those who have also believed in Him down through the ages.
- **New heavens and new earth:** We enjoy serving God dwelling in heaven with God at the New Jerusalem.
- Praise Him for calling you out of the darkness of your sin into His light.
- Thank Him for saving you from His wrath.
- Thank Him for saving you from what you would have become had He not delivered you from your previous course of life.
- Praise God for all that His salvation will do in your life.

Day 40: Works: Scriptures

Scriptures: 2 Timothy 3:16

> **2 Timothy 3:16,17**
> *All Scripture is inspired by God and profitable for teaching, for reproof, for correction, for training in righteousness; so that the man of God may be adequate, equipped for every good work.*

- Thank Him for communicating clearly to us in the Bible.
- Thank Him for the inerrancy of the Bible.
- Thank Him for helping your understand the Bible.

> **John 17:17**
> *Sanctify them in the truth;*
> *Your word is truth.*

Day 41: Overall Gratefulness of God

Overall gratefulness for all God is and has provided

1 Corinthians 4:7
And what do you have that you did not receive? But if you did receive it, why do you boast as if you had not received it?

- Thank God for what He has provided to you.
- Thank Him for providing a way to have relationship with Him through Jesus Christ's life, death, and resurrection.
- Thank Him for your life, soul, spirit, and body.
- Thank Him for your marriage, singleness, or future marriage.
- Thank Him for everything in your home.
- Thank Him for your family.
- Thank Him for your work.
- Thank Him for your church.
- Thank Him for your money and possessions.
- Thank Him for your community, region, and/or country.
- Thank Him for your friends.
- Thank Him for your enemies – those who oppose you.

Conclusion

Praising God touches the face of God. You have experienced what it means to enter into His presence praising the Lord God Almighty. Through these spiritual praise exercises you have been able to learn the self-revelation of God in the Scriptures. More importantly, you have interacted with God Himself.

There are few things that touch the spiritual world more directly and quickly than praising God. My hope for you is that by working through this book you have been changed by your contact with God and that you will never recover from that change.

I hope that you have had the wonder of doing some of these exercises with a group and some by yourself. Most people suggest that the two experiences are different and powerful in their own right.

If you have pushed through these exercises as an individual, let me suggest that you gather a group sometime within the next six months and do it as a group.

If you have moved through these exercises with a group, let me suggest that within the next six months you do them as an individual.

It can also be a wonderful thing to use these exercises as a part of the season of Lent (the forty days before Easter) or Advent (the month before Christmas).

Appendix: Why do we need to pray?

Why do we need to pray, work, and do the thousand other things that are required to get by in this world if there is an omnipotent God?

God could clearly make everything in our world complete and perfect, so that we do not have to do anything. But He has chosen through His infinite wisdom to leave many things unfinished. He wants us involved in the outworking of the completed project. Look at the nature of the world that God has created. Some things are complete and many things about our individual human lives are incomplete. It is helpful to notice that God purposely creates unfinished projects that we as humans must complete. He seems to do this so that we get involved and have ownership in our life and our world.

Our whole life is an unfinished project that can go in a lot of different directions. He has not predetermined everything we will do with our life (even though He does know). Our life is an opportunity that He gives us to choose to use the talents, skills, relationships, and situations that come our way to build a life that blesses Him and gives us satisfaction. Those people who moan and whine that life is not fair because someone else has less difficulties or more money at the start of life, often do not realize that life is an unfinished project that God wants you to build out with Him guiding the decisions that you make. We want God to give us a brand new house or a functioning business with lots of profits. But He doesn't do that , He give us the opportunity for a great house and the opportunity to build a great business. Prayer is one of the ingredients that you and I add to project. If we add it then the project goes better and further, if we don't then some of the potential of the opportunity is missed. If you wait for God or someone else to give you finished opportunities to enjoy, inhabit, or consume, your life will be miserable. We know that this is true by the overwhelming percentages of those with huge trust funds who lead shallow and meaningless lives. They do not have to strive, pray, communicate, work for anything. It is handed to them and it destroys the wonder of their life in many cases. It is in the building, designing, creating, testing, and working that makes life wonderful and significant. This is true of every part of life. This is the way that God made the life of humans.

Let's take a look at a few examples. The nature of relationships is that they are unfinished projects and must be completed by our communication, service, care, patience, and the like. God could have made us so that we did not need to communicate through external speech, but He did not because He wanted us to have to build the relationship through our speaking and listening to the other person. It is required. We cannot read each other's thoughts. We must talk to another person to have a relationship.

Children are another unfinished project that God planned into our world. He could have started the world with every person beginning as completely helpless dependent babies and grow up through an 18-to-25 year process requiring other adult involvement. Other species God created have litters and the parents walk away within weeks of the birth to never see the progeny again. He specifically designed child rearing as an unfinished project which will take years of investment on the parent's part. This is a tremendous amount of work, but raising children well brings a satisfaction that is very hard to put into words. God designed human life as an unfinished project that goes better when the parents put in lots of time, planning, prayer, communication and love.

The need for prayer is another unfinished project that God has purposely built into every person's time line. God could have made the world any way that He wanted. He could have had the things that we needed just show up at the exact time and place that they were going to be needed, but He did not. He decided that some things will show up without our involvement but many blessing, relationships, accomplishments, opportunities and joys will not show up unless we pray. There are many things that God will do without prayer, but there are many things in each of our individual lives that He will not do unless we pray. Our prayer is an essential element in accomplishing our highest potential.

Even God's answers to our prayers are often unfinished projects. He wants us to learn something, develop something, invest in something, and sense something by completing the project that comes as an answer to prayer. When I prayed for a wife and a great marriage, God answered my prayer with a wonderful young woman and the possibility of a great marriage. He did not give me a robotic wife who was already the perfect mate. And I was not the perfect husband who always did the right thing. We had to work at it, pray with each other, apologize and grow together to fulfill the promise of the great marriage that God heard in my prayer.

Remember that He can do anything He wants and yet He still sends unfinished projects that have "some assembly required." This is for our benefit not His. We gain and grow and become something by throwing ourselves into the projects that He obviously wants us to be a part of. If He did not then we would be like the boy who sought to help the butterfly out of the chrysalis. He cut the cocoon open and released the butterfly only to discover that the butterfly needed to push against the sides of the cocoon to force blood into its wings and strengthen the muscles of the wing. Because He eliminated the struggle, the butterfly had useless wings and soon died. God knows what we need more than we do, and He sends these work projects and opportunities for us to become all that He planned for us.

In the Garden of Eden before the fall of mankind into sin, the life that God gave Adam and Eve was full of unfinished projects. They had to tend and keep the garden, name the animals, eat, sleep, etc. Therefore God's infinite wisdom designs unfinished projects for us so that our lives will have meaning, purpose, and satisfaction. When sin entered the picture and man became a selfish, rebellious creature, the unfinished assignments of God did not stop. They are now interrupted by the imperfect and selfish actions of humanity and angels.

One of the ways we finish the projects that God gives us is by praying. He has specifically designed our lives and our world to not work in optimum ways without consulting and praying to Him. Therefore pray and keep praying. Jesus tells us to pray so that we do not faint.

Small Group Materials

There are six to eight weeks in this small group. This small group is designed as an active small group. The members of the small group must participate in the daily activities of prayer and praise or the group will not work out well. This 40 day adventure is six weeks of daily activities. This group is designed for the learning and growing to come during the experiencing of God through the praise assignments and the opportunity to talk about it the group time.

Over the course of the six to eight weeks the group will put an emphasis on all of the purposes of a dynamic church: Evangelism, Discipleship, Worship, Fellowship and Compassion. Each week will move through four of the five purposes. It is recommended to have a week where the whole group goes together and serves at some kind of service project. Most churches will have a list of recommended compassion and/or service organization.

Week 1: Introductions and Touching the Face of God
Week 2: Touching the Face of God
Week 3: Touching the Face of God
Week 4: Touching the Face of God
Week 5: Touching the Face of God
Week 6: Touching the Face of God
Week 7: Compassion or Social Justice project
Week 8: Celebration of the group

Some groups put the Compassion project in week 4 to make it an integral part of the group life.

Week 1

Start the group in prayer.

Introduction
Let everyone introduce themselves.
Tell us your name and anything else about yourself you want us to know.

Evangelism Section: 5 -10 minutes
Ask the members of the group, "Did anyone get a chance to share their faith during this last week?"

If someone did then let them share.

If no one did then ask if they would be willing to pray this prayer, "Dear Lord, I am willing to share my faith this next week. If you want me to share my faith, please have someone come up to me and ask me. If you do not then I do not have to share." In Jesus Christ name Amen.

Discipleship portion: 20-40 minutes
Pass out the books and/or make sure that people already have them.

The 40 Days of Adoring God moves the participants through the five basic aspects of God as described in the Bible. There is something powerful that takes place when individuals and groups take the time to praise God for who He is.

The Scriptures tell us that God is not like us and that the best ways to describe Him to us is through five basic aspects of His being:

His Essence
His Attributes
His Nature
His Names
His Works

Do a brief overview of these five elements and what pages in the book that particular aspect begins upon.

Give a sentence or two explaining each of these aspects of God. Do not try and teach through this material, instead just make sure that people are familiar with these descriptions and their basic meaning.

God describes Himself in the Bible in terms of five aspects of His being:

- His Essence:
  - o Infinite, Self-Existent, Spirit
- His Attributes:
  - o Omniscient; Omnipresent; Omnipotent, Immutable
  - o Holy, Righteous, Good, Merciful, Longsuffering, Truth, Sovereign
- His Nature:
  - o Father, Son, and Holy Spirit
- His Names:
  - o God, Lord, Lord of Hosts, Most High, Jesus, Savior, Christ, I AM, Almighty, The Holy One
- His Works:
  - o Creation, Exodus, Bible, Salvation

The group is an active participatory group. Each day the members of the group will do that days praise assignment. They will complete the praise assignment at some time during the day, making a few notes about what they did and how the time went.

Worship portion: 20-40 minutes
Ask each person to turn to page 11.

Spend the next 20-40 minutes praising God out loud in the group. This does not have to be loud or emotional just sincere reflection on the truths about God on page 11. I realize that this may be a little intimidating at first, but it is very easy to tell God that you think it is wonderful that He is a particular way.

People should feel free to jump in and thank God for the elements of His being that strike them. Some groups move through the material in order, giving people time to praise God for an element. Then they move on when everyone seems done.

It will be surprising how quickly time goes by once the process gets started. No one individual should dominate the prayer time, but everyone should get a chance to pray a sentence or two. Keep the prayer time moving by encouraging lots of people to praise. Enjoy the collective praying process.

This first week of praising the Lord in a group, breaks that ice about praying out loud in a group. If you have more than twelve people in the group then divide people into groups of three and have the smaller group be its own prayer circle. The point is to have everyone start praying. If there are too many people in the group some people will not pray at all.

Fellowship Portion: 5-30 minutes
Ask each individual for a prayer request for themselves.
This is not a time to ask for other people, the request must be for the individual themselves. If they do not have a personal pray request then the members of the group can pray anything they would like for that person.

Close in Prayer
Have some refreshments for people to enjoy.

Week 2

Start the group in prayer.

Introduction
Let everyone introduce themselves again or have name tags.
Tell us your name and anything else about yourself you want us to know.

Evangelism Section: 5 -10 minutes
Ask the members of the group, "Did anyone get a chance to share their faith during this last week?"
If someone did then let them share.
If no one did then ask if they would be willing to pray this prayer, "Dear Lord, I am willing to share my faith this next week. If you want me to share my faith, please have someone come up to me and ask me. If you do not then I do not have to share." In Jesus Christ name Amen.

Worship portion: 20-40 minutes
Enjoy the collective praying process.
The members of the small group should praise the Lord using all the material of the last week and today's element .

Discipleship portion: 20-40 minutes
It is important to let people talk about what happened when they spent the time each day in prayer. It is very likely that people will have powerful times experiencing God.

Which of the days were the most meaningful?

What did you do?

What happened when you did that?

What did you learn about God?

What did you sense God was communicating to you?

What do you need God to be for you of what you learned?

Fellowship Portion: 5-30 minutes
Ask each individual for a prayer request for themselves.
This is not a time to ask for other people, the request must be for themselves.
If they do not have a personal pray request then the members of the group can pray anything they would like for that person.

Close in Prayer
Have some kind of refreshment for people to enjoy.

Week 3

Start the group in prayer.

Introduction
Let everyone introduce themselves again or have name tags.
Tell us your name and anything else about yourself you want us to know.

Evangelism Section: 5 -10 minutes
Ask the members of the group, "Did anyone get a chance to share their faith during this last week?"
If someone did then let them share.
If no one did then ask if they would be willing to pray this prayer, "Dear Lord, I am willing to share my faith this next week. If you want me to share my faith, please have someone come up to me and ask me. If you do not then I do not have to share." In Jesus Christ name Amen.

Worship portion: 20-40 minutes
Enjoy the collective praying process.
The members of the small group should praise the Lord using all the material of the last week and today's element.

Discipleship portion: 20-40 minutes
It is important to let people talk about what happened when they spent the time each day in prayer. It is very likely that people will have powerful times experiencing God.

Which of the days were the most meaningful?

What did you do?

What happened when you did that?

What did you learn about God?

What did you sense God was communicating to you?

What do you need God to be for you of what you learned?

Fellowship Portion: 5-30 minutes
Ask each individual for a prayer request for themselves.
This is not a time to ask for other people, the request must be for themselves.
If they do not have a personal pray request then the members of the group can pray anything they would like for that person.

Close in Prayer
Have some kind of refreshment for people to enjoy.

Week 4

Start the group in prayer.

Introduction
Let everyone introduce the person to their left.
Tell us your name and anything else about yourself you want us to know.

Evangelism Section: 5 -10 minutes
Ask the members of the group, "Did anyone get a chance to share their faith during this last week?"
If someone did then let them share.
If no one did then ask if they would be willing to pray this prayer, "Dear Lord, I am willing to share my faith this next week. If you want me to share my faith, please have someone come up to me and ask me. If you do not then I do not have to share." In Jesus Christ name Amen.

Worship portion: 20-40 minutes
Enjoy the collective praying process.
The members of the small group should praise the Lord using all the material of the last week and today's element.

Discipleship portion: 20-40 minutes
It is important to let people talk about what happened when they spent the time each day in prayer. It is very likely that people will have powerful times experiencing God.

Which of the days were the most meaningful?

What did you do?

What happened when you did that?

What did you learn about God?

What did you sense God was communicating to you?

What do you need God to be for you of what you learned?

Fellowship Portion: 5-30 minutes
Ask each individual for a prayer request for themselves.

This is not a time to ask for other people, the request must be for themselves.

If they do not have a personal pray request then the members of the group can pray anything they would like for that person.

Close in Prayer

Week 5

Start the group in prayer.

Introduction
Let everyone introduce someone else in the group.
Tell us their name and something else we did not know.

Evangelism Section: 5 -10 minutes
Ask the members of the group, "Did anyone get a chance to share their faith during this last week?"
If someone did then let them share.
If no one did then ask if they would be willing to pray this prayer, "Dear Lord, I am willing to share my faith this next week. If you want me to share my faith, please have someone come up to me and ask me. If you do not then I do not have to share." In Jesus Christ name Amen.

Worship portion: 20-40 minutes
Enjoy the collective praying process.
The members of the small group should praise the Lord using all the material of the last week and today's element.

Discipleship portion: 20-40 minutes
It is important to let people talk about what happened when they spent the time each day in prayer. It is very likely that people will have powerful times experiencing God.

Which of the days were the most meaningful?

What did you do?

What happened when you did that?

What did you learn about God?

What did you sense God was communicating to you?

What do you need God to be for you of what you learned?

Fellowship Portion: 5-30 minutes
Ask each individual for a prayer request for themselves.

This is not a time to ask for other people, the request must be for themselves.

If they do not have a personal pray request then the members of the group can pray anything they would like for that person.

Close in Prayer
Have some kind of refreshment for people to enjoy.

Week 6

Start the group in prayer.

Introduction

Let everyone introduce God to the group, the most intense and amazing things about God that has struck them over these last six weeks.

Tell us your name and anything else about yourself you want us to know.

Evangelism Section: 5 -10 minutes

Ask the members of the group, "Did anyone get a chance to share their faith during this last week?"

If someone did then let them share.

If no one did then ask if they would be willing to pray this prayer, "Dear Lord, I am willing to share my faith this next week. If you want me to share my faith, please have someone come up to me and ask me. If you do not then I do not have to share." In Jesus Christ name Amen.

Worship portion: 20-40 minutes

Enjoy the collective praying process.

The members of the small group should praise the Lord using all the material of the last week and today's element.

Discipleship portion: 20-40 minutes

It is important to let people talk about what happened when they spent the time each day in prayer. It is very likely that people will have powerful times experiencing God.

Which of the days were the most meaningful?

What did you do?

What happened when you did that?

What did you learn about God?

What did you sense God was communicating to you?

What do you need God to be for you of what you learned?

Fellowship Portion: 5-30 minutes
Ask each individual for a prayer request for themselves.
This is not a time to ask for other people, the request must be for themselves.
If they do not have a personal pray request then the members of the group can pray anything they would like for that person.

Close in Prayer
Have some kind of refreshment for people to enjoy.

Compassion Week / Farewell Week
As a group do a compassion project together.

Preaching Materials

This material can be a part of a sermon series in which the Pastor explores the aspects of God's being. The following are ideas for various sermon series to kick off a group like this.

The following are six different approaches to tie this individual and small group material to the preaching of this material.

  1. Pick six or seven specific verses and preach those

  2. Take the five different topics developed each one of these in a sermon, with two weeks being used on the attributes

  3. Take six or seven different narrative passages in the Scriptures that bring out six or seven different aspects of God.

  4. Spend six or seven weeks in one passage such as Exodus 34:7-8; 1 Timothy 6:10-13

  5. Preach the topic that is discussed on the particular day in the book that your people will be going through that Sunday.

  6. Preach one sermon about God at the beginning of the series to launch the series and then let the small groups cover the rest of the material.

Other materials by Gil Stieglitz

BOOKS
Becoming a Godly Husband

Becoming a Godly Wife (with Dana Stieglitz)

Going Deep In Prayer: 40 Days of In-Depth Prayer

They Laughed When I Wrote Another Book About Prayer, Then They Read It: How To Make Prayer Work

Marital Intelligence: A Foolproof Guide for Saving and Strengthening Marriage

Mission Possible: Winning the Battle over Temptation

Leading a Thriving Ministry: 10 Indispensable Leadership Skills

Spiritual Disciplines of a C.H.R.I.S.T.I.A.N.: Intensive Training in Christian Spirituality

VIDEOS
Growing a Healthy and Vibrant Church

Marital Intelligence: There are Only Five Problems in Marriage

AUDIO
The Ten Commandments

God's Principles for Handling Money

Becoming a Godly Parent

If you would be interested in having Dr. Gil Stieglitz
speak to your group, you can contact him through the web site
www.ptlb.com.

CPSIA information can be obtained at www.ICGtesting.com
Printed in the USA
269643BV00001B/312/P